40 YEARS IN THE PSYCHOTHERAPIST'S CHAIR

A PERSONAL GUIDE TO PSYCHOLOGICAL GROWTH AND PSYCHOTHERAPY

DOUG FAVERO PH.D.

PUBLISHED BY IELA

First Edition
ISBN 978-1-66784-894-5
Published by IELA- ImagesEverything-Los Angeles
3666 Guerneville Rd. Santa Rosa, CA 95401
www.iela.net

Printed and bound in the United States of America
Cover and interior design by Thomas Gaebel

Cover: Voyage of Life: Childhood by Thomas Cole, 1801 - 1848
Courtesy National Gallery of Art, Washington D.C. USA

TO THE MEMORY OF

Joe and Babe, my parents and first teachers

Harold Lindner, my long-term therapist

Louise de Leeuw, my colleague and dear friend

CONTENTS

VISIONS OF ABUNDANCE

"My grandmother Gogo taught me to greet strangers thus: When the stranger asks, 'How are you?' you should respond with great care, 'I am well as long as you are well.'"

— ELIZABETH NYAMAYARO (contemporary) childhood memory

"Just now I am thinking of the summer I became eleven years old. From early springtime until the snows fell there was something new and stirring each day, and the summer was very fine. Meat was fat and plentiful when the days began to grow shorter. Ripe plums were thick on the trees, and black chokecherries bent the bushes with their weight."

— PLENTY-COUPS (1848-1932) childhood memory

"When I left my high school teaching career to become a psychotherapist, my first clients were long-term residential patients at Washington's St. Elizabeth's Hospital. Even though my client Anita was diagnosed as highly delusional, we had good sessions. One day, she told me that she had been hospitalized for forty-eight years and wanted to give some Christmas cheer to those who had helped her. I reminded her that it was only August, so we had plenty of planning time. 'I'm on the Julian calendar,' she replied, 'we should do this right now! Isn't forty-eight years of waiting long enough?' "

— DOUG FAVERO early career memory

"Our mother was an exuberant social dancer from her school years on. But in the last years of her life, she had a number of falls and bone breaks that took her out of the action. In her hundredth year, I accompanied her to see her doctor and friend, Dr. Bill George. She asked him why she had developed the habit of touching her thumbs to the other four fingers of each hand over and over again. 'Babe,' he replied, 'you've been a dancer your whole life. Now that you can't get out onto the floor anymore, you're dancing with your fingers.' She liked that explanation."

— DOUG FAVERO recent family memory

ACKNOWLEDGMENTS

I thank my colleagues who reviewed drafts of the following questions and answers and gave me helpful input. I am also grateful to those and other colleagues and friends who contributed insights about psychological growth and/or psychotherapy included in the Quotations at the end of each section.

I want to single out my colleague Stephen Stein Ph.D. for mentoring me throughout my entire career.

I am grateful to Elissa Favero for editing and encouraging me as I began writing, to Jan Phillips and David Oldfield for inspiring me toward the end of my writing, to Thomas Gaebel for getting me across the production finish line with intelligence and grace, and to Mitchell Story for his mighty help throughout the whole process of writing and publishing.

I honor my outstanding siblings, Phil Favero and Patti Fleck, and their spouses, for always deepening my understanding of what is important in life, and thus what is important in therapy. Not surprisingly, all of their children have ended up with careers in the helping professions.

Carl Rogers' (1902-1987) and Carl Jung's (1875-1961) respective insights about psychological growth have guided me from the beginning of my work as a therapist. Rogers gave me the tools to confidently begin seeing clients, and he has been with me in spirit as I've met every new client since. Jung has led me to go deep and high with clients who want the "full experience."

I also bow to the inspiring artist Thomas Cole (1801-1848) whose "Voyage of Life" guides us through these pages; and to the wonderful contemporary United Nations advisor Elizabeth Nyamayaro; and to the great twentieth century Apsaalooke chief Plenty-Coups (1848-1932). Their lives and work teach us how to heal in community.

I am especially grateful to my past and current clients. Your trust in me has given my life one of its deepest meanings. May your days always lean toward joy!

INTRODUCTORY LETTER

Dear Reader:

The twenty Questions and Answers that follow are reflections on psychological growth and on psychotherapy. For each of them in turn, I assume the voice of an interested reader, ask a question, offer a response, and then pose a return question or two to you.

While influenced by scholarly research and best practice tenets, my responses are in the end my own personal impressions, intuitions, and opinions distilled over forty years of conducting an adult psychotherapy practice in Washington, D.C. They are addressed from a generalist to the general reader who is curious about furthering personal growth, engaging in psychotherapy, and/or becoming a therapist.

My desire is that what you read here will reinforce your hope and encourage you to celebrate your unique life.

P.S.: If you are in an emotional emergency, please call the National Suicide Prevention Hotline (at 988, or 800-273-8255) or text the Crisis Text Line (text "Start" to 741-741) for immediate, confidential, and free help from a trained listener.

Best regards,

Doug Favero

PART ONE

PSYCHOLOGICAL GROWTH

CHAPTER ONE

LIFE STAGES

QUESTION #1

What are the stages of a human life, and what are some of the opportunities and challenges of each stage?

ANSWER #1

We human beings have always been fascinated with how our lives proceed from birth to death.

In ancient times, The Riddle of the Sphinx was, "What goes on four feet in the morning, two feet at noon, and three feet in the evening?" Those who understood that this creature is none other than ourselves—crawling as babies, walking on our own two feet as youths and adults, and leaning on a cane as oldsters—could disempower the fierce guardian of the road to wisdom.

In our own times, developmental thinkers have formulated detailed human life stage theories and outlines. Jean Piaget

(1896-1980), for example, addresses the human child's cognitive development; Erik Erikson (1902-1994) talks about the steps of a person's psychosocial development from infancy to old age; Abraham Maslow ((1908-1970) lays out our hierarchy of needs from the most basic to the most elevated; and Lawrence Kohlberg (1927-1987) speaks to the gradual unfolding of our sense of morality.

The landscape and history painter Thomas Cole (1801-1848) beautifully illustrates the stages of a human life in his four painting series done in the 1840's called "The Voyage of Life: Childhood, Youth, Manhood, and Old Age." His large and vividly painted canvases of a single human's boat journey down a winding river to the sea—guarded and guided by an angel—hang together in a small gallery of their own in Washington D.C.'s National Gallery of Art. I have visited them many times over the years to remind myself of the opportunities and challenges of the ever-moving experience that we call a human life.

Cole's first painting introduces an innocent and confident child heading off in a beautiful little boat on inviting waters with his glorious guardian angel at his back. Cole herein illustrates the unbounded enthusiasm associated with a "good enough" childhood.

The child's elation and fascination with the world serve

as the energy engine not just for the early years, but for ALL of the years of a human life. When our one hundred year old mother was in her last months, she told us that her mother, Margaret—dead for almost fifty years then —was "with me all the time now," evoking in my mother's memory how she had been the apple of Margaret's eye and providing her with a certain buoyancy to the final day of her life.

Since the human infant comes into the world highly dependent on parents and others, a crucial development in the first stage of life is acquiring exploration and self-care skills. This occurs through both child play, and the beginnings of informal and formal education. Be it learning how to crawl, how to ride a bike, how to brush ones teeth, or how to write a story, skills acquisition gives the child a growing confidence that they have the personal power to self-propel, solve problems, and bring tasks and interpersonal situations to fruition.

I was given a great gift during our early covid-19 sheltering months of 2021 in the birth of two healthy infants to close friends: little Zuri in Washington, D.C. and little Emma in Columbia, Missouri. As I held each of them in my arms for the first time, I experienced the opposite of the necessary carefulness we practice during a pandemic. Their cuddling, smiling, squirming and babbling were non-self-conscious expressions of life unbounded. These latest additions to our human family expect to be heard, seen, and responded to. They seem to be saying, "I belong here! I know the world loves me!"

Cole's second life stage, "Youth," illustrates what we commonly refer to as the adolescent and early adulthood years. This second painting introduces a strapping young man whose angel moves off to the side and waves him on as he pursues a perfect temple in the sky. Adolescence and young adulthood—the drama of which most of us older adults can still remember well, I'm sure—is typically characterized by angst and rebellion, as well as by idealism. Physical growth and new hormonal production often lead the teenager to feel awkward in their own body at the same time as they are coming to recognize the underbelly of parents, teachers and institutions that they may have heretofore thought of as perfect. All of this prepares the adolescent to critique the status quo and eventually leave the cocoon of the parental home and local schools to find a place in the wider world, which very well might include emotional and physical intimacy with others and even a (first) bonded intimate relationship.

The great opportunity and challenge of this second stage of life is to find a way to make a Hero's Journey, not just choosing a one-size-fits-all adventure off of someone else's rack, but tailor-making an adventure based on one's own special aptitudes and values.

I chatted recently with an old friend who enjoys musing about personal and interpersonal dynamics in the way many therapists and educators do. I asked her if her closely aligned sixteen year old daughter has her same interest in speculating about what makes people tick. "Not quite," smiled my friend, "she's got the mind of a scientist. She loves to engage me in talk about car exhaust omissions and the relative dangers to the climate of the various polluters." Maybe young Miel's adventures in life, I thought as I listened, will revolve around getting our world out of this climate-change mess that could absolutely do us in without some heroic adventurers spurring us on to change the way we develop and use energy.

The day before that conversation, I met a twenty-eight year old friendly stranger at a picnic table outside of the Red Lodge, Montana taco restaurant that I'd visited for lunch. Sam turned out to be a cross-country backpacker who was in the process of stringing together solo wilderness hikes from his native Massachusetts all throughout the West. He told me that he wants to experience the big outdoors before settling into life with a partner and a home state job. I can only imagine what his bravery is teaching him about both his own physical and emotional capacities as well as the contours of the natural world.

Sixteen year old Miel and twenty-nine year old Sam, stand at the early and late junctures of the second stage of life. As they engage their respective adventures, they will, in traditional Hero Journey language, find their "Spiritual Mother" or "Spiritual Father" and bring back a boon of new energy and knowledge to their respective communities of origin. Simultaneously—and probably unwittingly—they are preparing themselves for all of the smaller, less glitzy hero's journeys each of us must make again and again throughout our lives if we are to be physically and emotionally well. The twenty year old Olympic sprinter's unbreakable will that pushes her to win a gold medal in her preferred race is the same will that will push her to complete a hike on the Appalachian Trail in late mid-life, and to make the transfer from bed to wheelchair in late old age.

In the third of Cole's paintings, which he calls "Manhood" but which in our age of more inclusive language we might call "Full Adulthood," our navigator's angel has become invisible to him. The sky has turned black, roiling waters are funneling his boat into a narrow passageway through treacherous terrain, and he is in a panicked prayer for mercy. We have come to the time of life in which the hyper-competitive order of "tooth and claw" often rules and "the survival of the fittest" often prevails in the scramble for resources and control, such that living can begin to feel weighty and even at times perilous.

In this mid-life stage—which can last for forty or more years—the focus, then, is in on climbing one's chosen ladder, on building one's household, business, and/or empire. While Cole chooses to illustrate the dark aspect of these activities, some other artist might have painted a scene extolling middle-age accomplishment. Think of the musician Ludwig Beethoven, for instance, who worked despite his deafness to create several of the greatest masterpieces of music ever written before dying at the age of fifty-seven; or think of the skilled politician and eventual statesman Franklin Delano Roosevelt who, despite being robbed of the use of his legs by polio, led our nation out of the Great Depression and through the catastrophes of World War II before he died of exhaustion and heart failure at sixty-three. In terms of nurturance, think of every good parent who raises a child from complete dependence to happy, productive interdependence; think of every good nurse and doctor who educates us on how to stay healthy and assists us through our medical crises; and think of every good teacher who lights up our curiosity, our appreciation of the past, and our sense of possibility and hope about our futures.

Fr. Don Talafous, a Benedictine monk who was one of my undergraduate college teachers and still now in his mid-nineties dispenses his mid-western brand of spiritual wisdom in daily email offerings from St. John's Abby in Minnesota, gives us the key to insuring that the middle years are healthy rather than horrific. He tells us that all of the earlier-stage preparation for full adulthood, "acquires meaning and purpose when…we begin to use our talents, our time, our achievement, our means and acquisitions, our skills, our patience, all our experience and know-how for others." Washington, D.C. physician Carlos Picone says it this way: "If we are always looking forward to give and not to receive, life becomes more pleasurable, and interactions fill up with meaning and relevance."

The opposite of Fr. Don's and Dr. Carlos' healthy adult is the figure we encounter in mythology by the name of Holdfast. Holdfasts have traditionally been seen as male, but in reality they can be of any gender. They are people who have reached adulthood and become powerful because of their money, family status, and/or fame, but because of their narcissism or their greed—both of which are, deep down, brands of unacknowledged and unhealed fear—cling to their purse strings and their podiums with white knuckles. Despite their privileged lives, they often feel misunderstood and besieged. They do not comprehend the stance of a Good Samaritan who sees humanity in the foreigner as well as in the compatriot.

We each have at least a little of Holdfast in us. The challenge of mid-life is to diminish our fears, and to use at least some of our talent and energy to turn the wheel of the common good. Contributions of the engaged, compassionate adult can be small acts of kindness toward self and others, as well as major gifts to the whole of society.

Elizabeth Nyamayaro, whose name I introduced in the

Visions of Abundance and Acknowledgement sections above, is a great example of a fearless and compassionate adult contributor to a broad swath of humanity. As a young girl, she literally lay dying of starvation on the scorched earth of her native draught-ridden Zimbabwe. She was eventually rescued by a woman in a blue uniform, whom she later came to know was a United Nations relief worker. Elizabeth determined that someday she, too, would work for the United Nations. With gargantuan personal courage and wit, she eventually found her way as a young adult to London, and then to New York, to pursue her dream. Her contributions have been many but none greater than leading the "HeForShe" program whose purpose is to engage men as well as women in the battle for gender equality where women are especially culturally disadvantaged.

We are blessed by the Elizabeth Nyamayaros of the world. They are flesh and blood reminders that we are most whole and dynamic when we see ourselves as parts of a network bigger than ourselves as individuals. Using an old Hindu image, we might then view ourselves as jewels in an immense net of jewels, each of us reflecting all of the other jewels and shining in brilliance alongside them.

Before we turn to the fourth stage of life, we should remind ourselves to refrain from judging a person's value by how long they live. People who pass away in one of the first three stages of life—not only assassinated heroes such as Jesus of Nazareth (c. 4 BCE- 30/33 CE), Martin Luther King Jr. (1929-1968), and Harvey Milk (1930-1978), but also young adults such as our soldiers who have died in our many wars, and our vital friends who died in the AIDS epidemic of the 1980's and 1990's and the covid-19 pandemic of today—merit our full attention and appreciation.

Many years ago now I joined the great Buddhist peace activist Thich Nhat Hanh and his Washington, D.C. followers in a silent walking meditation from Arlington Cemetery to the Viet Nam Memorial. When we arrived at the famous Maya Lin wall, he reached out and put a single finger on a single engraved name of one of our lost soldiers, thereby signifying the unique importance of each and every one of them.

My colleague Jody Reiss pays tribute to a number of her young adult clients who died in the AIDS epidemic in her beautiful book "Looking Back: AIDS Tales and Teaching." Focusing on the death of her client David, she writes: "He was just 25. He had lived in a small room in a small flat on Cortland Avenue and he died so quickly his father missed his final days. The father came afterward, handsome, blond, not yet 50, beaten down but trying to remain stoic for his young son, David's 5-year-old half-brother he'd brought with him."

I, myself, lost two great friends to the AIDS epidemic. They were John Maddix, a talented therapist, and Frank Blanco, a magical playwright. They died in their early forties much as they had lived—with humor, growing wisdom, and an appreciation of mystery.

I especially think of John and Frank when Washington's flowering cherry trees bloom each spring. I remember Frank's ecstasy one March afternoon of the year he died when I rescued him from his hospital room and took him for a little spin around the blooming Tidal Basin trees. "GO GIRLS!" he grinned as he stared out of his passenger seat window at the unabashedly beautiful unfurling blossoms, "GO GIRLS!' My writing in this chapter is dedicated to my friend Frank who could write me under the table but would be smiling approvingly at my efforts here. He always encouraged me to be brave.

In Thomas Cole's fourth and final painting, our boat rider is now clearly an old man. He approaches the confluence of the river on which he has spent his life, and the open sea. The sky is brightening. His guardian angel is again clearly visible and encouraging. Our navigator has fought the good fight and is nearing the end of his voyage, the end of his life, in a state of peace, maybe even in ecstasy.

The opportunities of older adulthood open up as a we become more skilled at stepping out of "doing mode' and entering "being mode." In terms of our inner-worlds, this is the time of life when we can come to a greater understanding of the meaning(s) of our unique journeys. It is also the time when we might deepen our gratitude for the gift of a human life we have been given. Think of it. We are the only creatures whom we know of to date who have an awareness of the mystery of this huge, magnificent, unfathomable universe which births us, sustains us, and takes us back into its bosom at our deaths.

In the outer world, the prime opportunity of the final stage of life is to utilize our acquired personal authority to guide and support the younger generations. Picture a gentle grandparent imparting wisdom to a rebellious or timid teenage grandchild in the patient manner that a more everyday-involved and everyday-responsible parent might not always be able to muster.

When Thomas Cole was painting—which was approximately twenty years before Abraham Lincoln (1809-1865) became President—a long life typically lasted for about "three score and ten," seventy years. These days, those of us who make it to seventy might hope for even several more decades of life beyond that traditional end point. I was recently talking to a good friend, Carl, who has made it into his eighties. He has the wonderful capacity to remember his nighttime dreams in great detail. He told me a dream that he'd had just the night before our conversation: "I, Carl, was my age. I was standing near a railroad track. I witnessed someone driving a large stake into the track bed. I became aware that I was receiving a 'spiritual transplant.' I came to understand that the only requirement from me to receive this gift was to be grateful to those who were giving it to me."

As I listened to my friend, I nodded in understanding. Each of us who wishes to remain dynamic in our lives, however long they last, needs a periodic spiritual transplant—an infusion of new energy and new hope. Carl had gotten one from his inner dream-maker the night before our conversation, and his telling of the tale to me inspired me to expect my own next one—from either an inner-world offering or from an outer-world experience—sometime soon.

Deep history gives us a role model for the fourth stage of life in the wonderful Buddha (circa 6th c. BCE). Two and a half millennia ago, he lived with zest past his early adulthood enlightenment, all the way to his mid-eighties, with the specific intention of helping people ease their suffering.

Closer to our own time, we have a dynamic model of eighty-some year old vitality and potency in the figure of early twentieth century Native American Chief Plenty-Coups of the Crow (Apsaalooke) people, whom I introduced in the Visions of Abundance and the Acknowledgement sections above. He came upon the scene as his people were being decimated by the loss of the once ubiquitous buffalo to white settler slaughters. And, as if the ensuing famine were not enough, the Crow people of that time were also being ravaged by a tuberculosis epidemic.

As Plenty-Coups' name implies, he had been a brave warrior in his young adult years. But now, in his later years, he took a cue from the scrappy little black and white chickadee bird, and from his own spiritual visions, to became a curious listener, a learner from mistakes of both the white invaders and his own people. In the words of philosopher/ psychiatrist Jonathon Lear (contemporary), Plenty-Coups introduced a "radical hope" to his people that allowed them to transition from their traditional nomadic hunting life to a more domestic life in a world dominated by white settler agriculture, without losing their dignity.

Plenty-Coup's ongoing legacy was recently brought home to me in a very personal way. On November 11, 2021, I was invited to meet up with a delegation of Crow people who had come from Montana to Washington D.C. to help our country celebrate the one hundred year anniversary of the dedication of the Tomb of the Unknown Soldier at Arlington Cemetery. One hundred years earlier, Plenty-Coups, in full traditional warrior dress, had represented all of the Nations of Native Americans at the dedication of the Tomb. Now, in the conversation that ensued between the delegation members and myself, I experienced the aliveness—the straightforwardness, honesty, humor, steadfastness, and dignity—of these descendents of the great chief.

My friend Lawrence Flat Lip is an Apsaalooke elder who

lives with his wife Jennifer and their family near Plenty
Coup's old house on Crow lands. He reminded me recently
that beckoning the powers of the spiritual world (BAA.
WAA.CHII.WEE.KIIK); believing in ones self-worth and
self-expectations; and learning patience are the best habits
of mind for navigating personal hardships, and for standing
ready to meet the unknowns toward which our world is
hurling.

My fellow elder and friend Lucille Olds speaks in her
beautiful poem below of the challenge of claiming and sharing
the kind of wisdom that emerges in us after having lived many
years of life in consciousness:

I have always been
Drawn to older people
Their kindness, their
Knowledge of life,
Their generosity of words,
Wisdom and stories.
Now I am one of them
But do I share
What I have learned
And is it truly wisdom?

Several months ago, I sat across the breakfast table from

15

a dear friend's mother, a very hardy ninety-seven year old woman with sparkling conversational skills and the unlikely first name of Mark. We had never met before, so she had some questions about me. Interspersed with these, she talked about her own lifelong passions, including devouring mystery novels and listening to the music of Bach.

Mark speculated about how it is that her dearest age-mate friend is a political conservative whereas she, herself, is an outspoken liberal. Coming to know that I am a psychologist, she asked me with a twinkle in her eye, "What's wrong with me? Many of the people surrounding me in my retirement community are just waiting to die, but I still have the mindset of a 35 year old." Then she answered her own question. "I have ten or twelve physical issues to deal with, but I don't hurt, so I can ignore them. I'm curious about things. I reach out."

Whichever stage of life you are in, dear reader, I hope that you, like Mark, will always be curious and ready to search out adventures beyond your close circle and known territory.

QUESTIONS FOR THE READER

Do the challenges and opportunities of life as outlined here mirror the realities of your own life? How might your own life differ from what you read here?

CHAPTER TWO
HAPPINESS

QUESTION #2

What have you learned in your years as a psychotherapist about what makes people happy?

ANSWER # 2

For starters, I've learned that happiness is not something we can chase, capture, and bottle. Rather, it appears to be a byproduct of fulfilling our vital needs, making some creative adventures for ourselves, and reaching out to others. It often seems to be associated with developing a life view that emphasizes ironic humor and playfulness, whatever particulars life is sending us at any given moment.

I have come to know, too, that happiness is sometimes—straight out—an unwarranted gift from the universe!

We humans have several basic needs that exist without ceasing from the moment we are born to the last breath we take. The first of these are our physical needs for unpolluted air, food, drink, sleep, and movement. The fulfillment of these physical basics leads us to our first and ongoing sense of wellbeing.

Concurrently, we have crucial psychological needs. We require a base of safety from which we can reach out for stimulation and adventure. We thrive when we have secure attachments to sources of unconditional love, and companionship, such that we can experience and eventually internalize a sense of stability and tolerate frustrations.

Hopefully, the child you once were experienced "good-enough-nurturing" such that you began satisfying your basic needs from your first days. But none of us gets through childhood perfectly protected and cared for. Every child has some kind of emotional burden to carry—visible or not—and thus every adult has some kind of story to tell and some kind of healing to do.

Once we consistently meet our first-order needs, exploring our particular talents and passions comes to the fore as a great source of happiness.

I, myself, for example, have focused throughout my life on academic and career achievement, with additional major interests in finding ways to act on my compassion for others, and on exploring my spirituality. I have not always been on point in climbing my ladders, being kind to others, and experiencing myself as a part of the big picture, but an interest in these three arenas seems to forever reappear and guide my next step.

Other folks I've come to know are more driven by being parents or mentors, artists or craftspeople, scientists or nature explorers, athletes or adventurers, thinkers, organizers, prophets etc. The psychological term "individuation" is relevant here. Life feels "right" when we identify and live out our particular aptitudes and interests.

When Stephen Speilberg recently re-created the 1961 great American film "West Side Story," he cast ninety year old Rita Moreno—who had played the young "Anita" in the original— as the wise elder "Valentina." Actresses Ariana DeBose and Rachel Zegler who play the young female leads in the new film, met Moreno for lunch during rehearsals and asked her for her views about their roles. Rather than schooling them in the 1961 interpretations, Moreno encouraged them to, "lean into everything that makes you unique." Upon hearing this, I nodded "yes." Our life journeys require us to learn from the past, but our richest expressions come from melding what we learn there into our unique inclinations and talents.

Creating a good relationship with TIME is another great

boon to our happiness. Becoming proficient in the use of left-brain-mediated "normal time" involves conscientiously utilizing the twenty-four hours of the day to work, play, and rest creatively and well. But our opportunities for time-related happiness are not complete unless we concurrently cultivate the right-brain-mediated "boundless time." In these experiences, we allow ourselves to become intrigued with compelling activities or reveries during which we "lose track of time," experience an absorption in something larger than ourselves, and thus evoke a sense of relaxation, and—if we open our minds and our hearts wide enough—a sense of compassionate wonder and awe. Living out a combination of left-brain and right-brain time experiences each day is a wonderful way to feel fulfilled.

And then teaching ourselves to live from playfulness and humor—rather than from fear and sadness—can make all of the difference in our felt quality of life. I have come to believe that the best question my late therapist Harold Lindner ever asked me was, "Doug, do you want to worry about your life, or celebrate your life?" Luckily I had acquired enough emotional intelligence by the time he asked me the question to answer, "I think I want to be happy."

For born worriers like me, or for people who tend toward depressive or angry moods, or even for folks who are superficially happy-go-lucky but actually living in avoidance or addiction, humor and playfulness can go a long way in helping us turn around even deeply entrenched negative thought and feeling patterns.

When I was a young teenager attending our three room Montana Catholic school, a man of great humor and joy—an elderly Cardinal by the name of Angelo Roncalli (1881-1963)—was elected pope. He took the name John XXIII, but he soon became known by his many fans of all faiths as Good Pope John. He was absolutely serious about bringing his church out of the self-righteous triumphalism that many of his predecessors touted, but what captivated Pope John watchers most on a daily basis was his joy.

Soon after his election, someone asked the portly John about his weight, and he laughed, "Well, I don't think we should think of papal elections as beauty contests." When someone asked him how many people worked in the Vatican, he replied, "Oh I'd say about half of the employees." And when the young, stylish and charismatic wife of the new American President John Kennedy—a world-wide phenomenon by the name of Jacqueline Kennedy—flew from Washington D.C. to the Vatican to pay a visit, John eschewed all formality and sped toward her with open arms and, "Jackie, Jackie, where have you been?"

Living in joy is not denying the sorrow, tentativeness, and shortness of human life. It is not being a marshmallow and avoiding a worthy fight. It is choosing sometimes to live in the comic mode rather than the tragic mode. It is chuckling at the inconsistencies and ironies that abound and surround us every day of our lives. It is choosing to not take ourselves too seriously and to sometimes be ready to be goofy, especially for love. It is incorporating the notion that we humans are a small and interdependent part of the universe rather than its rightful masters. It is being simultaneously strong and humble.

In terms of living in both strength and humility, Pope John said it in these words: "Everyday is a good day to be born, and everyday is a good day to die."

QUESTIONS FOR THE READER

The American mythologist Joseph Campbell (1904-1987) advises us to be detectives in search of our own souls. "If you follow your bliss," he tells us, "you put yourself on a kind of track that has been there all the while waiting for you...When you can see that, you begin to meet people who are in the field of your bliss, and they open the doors to you." Can you identify any of your thoughts, feelings, or activities that lead you to experience what Joseph Campbell calls "bliss?"

Also, the American humanistic psychologist Abraham Maslow (1908-1970) tells us that we are all capable of "peak experiences" in which ego is transcended and, "the whole universe is perceived as an integrated and unified whole." Are you aware as of having experienced such joyful boundlessness? If not, would you like to?

CHAPTER THREE
SPIRITUALITY

QUESTION #3

What is spirituality? Is it accessible to me?

ANSWER #3

Some people see themselves as distinctly separate individuals living largely self-determined lives in a basically material world. A number of these individuals claim "good" for themselves and their close associates while projecting "evil" onto the stranger and the foreigner.

But throughout the millennia of our history, we humans have evolved a higher consciousness that can take us beyond self-protective, self-limiting identifications to an awareness that we are each connected to "other" and "all."

Spirituality involves using this great human capacity to get into a respectful "I-Thou" relationship with seen and unseen elements of life that exist beyond our narrow first-concerns. It is even possible for us to reach a point where our primary identification is with the whole of humanity (deceased, living, and yet to be born) and our whole world.

Most spiritual people are attracted to the "Good Samaritan" stance of caring for others in need. The caring can be directed toward other people, other forms of life, and even the planet itself. Some of our dearest hidden acts of kindness as well as our greatest humanitarian initiatives flow from folks who are living out this orientation.

Some spiritual people also nurture an intense personal awareness of the source and sustaining force of the universe, often referred to as God. The thirteenth century Persian poet Rumi wrote: "Don't be the rider who gallops all night and never sees the horse that is underneath him." Mystics among us live out a daily heart relationship with God as if they were an intimate family member or lover.

People who think deeply about their spirituality realize that egoistic urges are, and to some degree necessarily are, alive inside each of us. These folks often engage in regular practices of self-reflection such as meditation, contemplative writing, centering prayer, spiritually oriented communion with other likeminded souls, and individual or group psychotherapy to keep themselves open to their "light" and honest about their "shadows."

The great religions offer us examples of stellar individuals who reached spiritual heights. Think of Moses, Jesus, Buddha, Mohammed, and Ramakrishna (1836-1886). But thoughtful students of religion such as the humanistic psychologist Abraham Maslow of the previous generation, and the artist and philosopher Jan Phillips of our own generation, caution us about deifying these great ones in such a way that, inadvertently or not, we set them apart from us and relieve ourselves of the hard work of journeying toward wholeness as they did. Jesus of Nazareth reminds us that the Kingdom of God begins within the hearts of each one of us who is leading a life oriented toward love.

Closer to our own era and home, outstanding spiritual Americans such as Abraham Lincoln, Martin Luther King Jr., the statesperson Barbara Jordan (1936-1996), and the capital punishment abolitionist Sister Helen Prejean (contemporary) come to mind. Each of these inspiring figures critiques the notion that earthly power is the be-all and end-all of human life, and promotes the primacy of love.

Psychological thinker Carl Jung was insightful about the relationship between love and power. "Where love reigns," he stated, "there is no will to power; and where the will to power is paramount, love is lacking. The one is but the shadow of the other." Writer Maya Angelou (1928-2014) speaks to us of the dynamics of love. "Love recognizes no barriers. It jumps hurdles, leaps fences, penetrates walls to arrive at its destination full of hope."

Some extraordinary people come to a full-blown vision of the oneness of humankind very early in life. The German-Dutch diarist Anne Frank, who lived from 1929 to 1945, dying at the age of fifteen, is a very famous example. She was one of the six million Jews and other "undesirables" whom the Nazis rounded up for elimination in 1930's and 1940's Europe. She, her sister Margot, and her mother Edith all died in the concentration camps of Bergen-Belsen and Auschwitz. Her father Otto Frank survived to eventually find and pass on the diary that his daughter had kept in the two years that the Frank family was in hiding before their arrest. While some of Anne's thoughts and feelings are those of a typical teenager individuating and asserting herself inter-personally, others rise to the level of a mature spirituality. She tells us, "Where there's hope, there's life. It fills us with fresh courage and makes us strong again." She reminds us that, "Human greatness does not lie in wealth or power, but in character and goodness." And she encourages us on with, "How wonderful it is that nobody need wait a single moment before starting to improve the world."

Some adults who eventually become outstanding spiritual people begin their lives with rough edges or—contrastingly—with a cautiousness about ruffling feathers. But they gradually rise above themselves to fight for their mature visions. They dream beyond the norms of their times. They shine bright lights onto the suffering of those in need, whom they think of as equals.

The scrappy New York journalist, social activist and love-driven Dorothy Day (1897-1980) had something important to say to all of us who aspire to live spiritually: "The greatest challenge of the day is how to bring about a revolution of the heart, a revolution that has to start with each one of us."

Constitutionally cautious El Salvadoran Archbishop Oscar Romero (1917-1980) accomplished such a revolution inside himself. Then, he preached an ever more urgent message of social justice to his countrymen. The country's oligarchy felt increasingly threatened and eventually hired a gunman to kill him. The deed was accomplished as Romero stood at the altar of a San Salvador hospital chapel, attended by campesinos, on March 24, 1980. Pope Francis declared Oscar Romero a martyr, and then a saint, thirty-eight years after his death.

Moving from the heroic expression of spirituality to its poetic expression, contemporary poet Mitchell Story in his beautiful poem "A Foyer," speaks about the nexus between life and death, between our bodily lives and the world of the spirit.

"A Foyer"
Stopping at country burying grounds
Or small town churchyards with their
Gardens of stones and cedars
And grass is a habit of my lifetime

They are peaceful and one can think
Yesterday on a low ridge above
A gently rolling brown and gray valley
Beside a small white house of the lord
On a blue sky December afternoon
With clouds in rows stretching forever

We found a family plot once enclosed
By single ceremonial iron bars held in by
Low limestone obelisks but the bars
Gone just holes left like eye sockets
Maybe the iron was needed in wartime

Had the family pulled them out with the
Hope their hard substance might ward off
A premature addition to the soil there
I'll ponder that one a long time
Maybe the mowers just got tired of them

But by my dreamtime twelve hours later
Those obelisks were marking the foyer
To a pavilion of glass in which I resided
The windows were clear as air and I could
Slide them up to smell a marvelous world

All around me were meticulously pruned
Roses and fragrant herbs between them
I was quite pleased with the plantings
I could see it would take work to maintain
Though I wouldn't need to worry about time

QUESTIONS FOR THE READER

Do you resonate with any of the traditionally honored "spiritual giants?"

Do you see yourself as a spiritual person? Why or why not? Can you identify spiritual elements in Mitchell Story's poem?

Could you write a few lines of your own prose or poetry that express some aspect of your own spirituality?

CHAPTER FOUR
OUR STORIES

QUESTION #4

I hear that psychological growth involves changing the stories we tell ourselves. Do you agree?

ANSWER #4

Yes, I do.

The wonderful children's book author Kate DiCamillo ("The Tiger Rising") tells us that healthy stories weave together the real joy—and the real terror—of our human lives, fitting the blend into an appropriate container such that we can bear and celebrate all of whom we are rather than deny, distort, or succumb to the most difficult parts.

But some of our own personal stories may not be so healthy. Interestingly, our skewed stories might be only one or two sentences long. "There is something shamefully wrong with me, and I need to hide it from the world," or, "Nothing is amiss here; I am perfectly happy," are examples of two not

31

uncommon stories that are distorted by being so extreme.

Our limiting stories often play and replay in our heads in a murky way—more or less outside of our awareness, or sometimes completely out of our awareness—so a first step toward changing them is identifying them more clearly.

Part of the identification process is straightforward. Just ask yourself what you most like and dislike about yourself; go historical with a question such as, "What is the deepest regret of my life?" or go futuristic with, "What is my wildest, craziest dream for myself?" In each case, the net you throw will haul up parts and pieces of your long-held stories as well as elements of your true nature. Sorting out one from the other can be hugely productive.

For searching the more remote crevices of your soul, you could make a practice of collecting and studying your dreams, or doing stints of spontaneous writing or mindfulness meditation. This kind of work yields the best results if we do it not just once, but consistently over a period of time. It gives our old stories the opportunity to gradually dislodge from the bedrock of the unconscious and surface into consciousness at their own pace.

Sometimes, though, without any planned effort, a story that we're unconsciously telling ourselves will emerge into consciousness in an interaction we are having with another person. As our mother got older, she became more direct in her communications with us, her three late middle-aged children. During one of her and my last Christmases together, we went to a restaurant that presented us with an unfamiliar menu. When we came to an entrée item that we were uncertain about, she said, "Ask the waiter." I replied, "Oh Mom, we can figure it out." She looked me in the eye: "You men! You can never ask for help." As the dinner progressed, I began to chuckle. Mom had called me out on one of my old stories. Despite being a therapist who is often focused on helping people open up about their vulnerabilities, in my hometown restaurant at that moment I was again the slight, quiet Montana boy who told himself that he just couldn't afford to call attention to his "weakness" by asking for help, especially from another man.

Additionally, from time to time, an up-to-date story of our true nature spontaneously emerges into view. This is a gift from our deep self. For instance, several years ago I was sitting alone in a reverie at a sun-streaming window in my office. Seemingly out of nowhere, a vision of a somewhat bruised but sweet man of a certain age popped into my head. I instantly felt a deep tenderness toward this imperfect being. I intuitively knew that he had suffered—especially in his earlier years when he had sometimes felt insecure and depressed and often chose, in response, to isolate himself. I knew that throughout his life he had sometimes been helpful to — and at others times insensitive to — others. I knew that through it all, though, he had believed in life and hope. I realized that this was an image-story of my current self seen through the lens of love.

QUESTIONS FOR THE READER

Physician-theologian Jeffrey Rediger M.D. (contemporary) researches physical and emotional healing. He tells us that our all-important immune systems can be bolstered by "understanding (ourselves) in an entirely new light," i.e., by altering our old, limiting stories about ourselves.

Are you aware of any less-than-true negative stories you tell yourself about yourself? Do they lead you to feel bad about yourself or stall you in making progress in life?

What is the truest story of your current self seen through the lens of love and thus infused with the tonic of hope?

CHAPTER FIVE
HEALTHY LIVING

QUESTION #5

What does an emotionally healthy life look like?

ANSWER #5

There are as many possible faces of an emotionally healthy life as there are humans who walk the face of the earth. Despite our commonalities, each of us, like the proverbial snowflake, has our own slightly unique design, our own special style of being whole. The great American sociologist Margaret Meade said it this way: "Always remember that you are absolutely unique. Just like everyone else."

Think of your favorite extrovert—maybe your Aunt Babe—and your favorite introvert—maybe your Uncle Joe— and notice their different ways of exhibiting confidence, their different styles of reaching toward others. Babe enjoys throwing big extended-family dinner parties in which participants can renew connections and express affections; Joe has to stiffen himself to get through Babe's parties, but he is absolutely comfortable having private conversations with his grocery store customers who have fallen on hard times and need to negotiate bill payments or have a bill forgiven.

But beneath our many different faces, healthy humans have universally shared inner-qualities. These include a robust acceptance of self and the world, tendencies toward both stability and flexibility, and a desire to reach toward others in goodwill.

I want to offer a sketch of a healthy human from my personal life, our aunt Cleonice (aka Cleo), who lived to the age of ninety-five and died in the year 2001. Her outer profile might run contrary to what you would on first blush think of as a fulfilled life par excellence, but she indeed lived one.

Cleo's family lost their father in a coal mine accident when she was in her early twenties. Rather than eventually marry and move out of the family home, she lived there as a single adult supporting her widowed mother who lived for another fifty years.

Professionally, Cleo was the hairdresser of choice in our little Montana town. Six days a week, fifty-two weeks a year—for almost sixty years—she welcomed her "patrons" with open arms at her Beauty Salon, after which she walked the six blocks back home to help keep the house and the garden. She never had a romantic partner or children. She had some inner fears and a few difficult people in her life.

Through it all, Cleo was happy! As a tween and teenager, I practiced my music on her old upright piano. As I played, I'd catch her out of the corner of my eye two rooms over stepping and clapping in joy. She sang and danced with gusto well into her nineties.

Sigmund Freud tells us that the mainstays of a good life are work and love. Cleo had a passion for the work that she practiced. When I opened my psychotherapy practice, I kidded her that while I hoped to give MY clients encouragement and a good ear, I knew that she gave HER patrons encouragement, a good ear, AND a great "do."

Cleo loved mightily. Her family members were central. Since I was one of her four nieces and nephews, I got the full embrace. For me the little boy, and then for me the man, Cleo conveyed trust that I knew what I was doing and that I would always find my way to do the right thing. I basked in her glow.

And Cleo cared about a very broad circle of people beyond close family. Way back in our mining town's early days, she befriended the sex workers whom she coiffed and thought of them as fellow struggling working women. And in my early life, she cared about the rodeo cowboys in their hats and boots who stepped into her shop because her haircuts were very reasonably priced (two bucks a shot), but mostly because Cleo made these men, and all of her customers, feel understood and special.

Cleo was not a Pollyanna. She saw people's shadows and could roll her eyes at them. But shadows were not what she sought out. Perhaps you've heard of people who make a game of trading insults for fun, playing "the dozens" game? Cleo turned that contest on its head. She was a trader of compliments. You could give her a bit of appreciation, but she would always turn that into an even more generous — and mostly true! — compliment back to you.

I was privileged to be with Cleo when she died. She had been in the hospital for a few weeks suffering from a deteriorating heart condition. I talked softly to her as she rested in semi-consciousness. Suddenly she opened her eyes, raised her head and shoulders off of her pillow, looked into deep space, inhaled with an extended and resounding "AH" and did not breathe out again. I held my great friend's hand. I smiled at her through tears that were suddenly streaming down my cheeks. It was as if in her final breath, Cleo broadened her already huge embrace to all and everything.

QUESTIONS FOR THE READER

Do you have a Cleo in your life? Or are you a Cleo to someone else? Either way, how does the relationship inspire and challenge you?

And what is your hope for yourself in your later years?

CHAPTER SIX
SELF HEALING

QUESTION #6

Do we have the power to heal ourselves? If so, how do we access it?

ANSWER #6

I believe that each of us humans has great reservoirs of natural growth and healing potential. Various therapies and health-promoting practices can show us how to shift this potential into enlightened and compassionate thoughts, emotions, and actions. By the way, mental health might be thought of as the ability to consistently tap into and actualize our healing potential in our daily lives.

There are a number of highly regarded paths to healing that come with traditions, lines of great teachers, and bodies of fellow practitioners. Let me list some of these with which I am most familiar with their intended goals. I will save the practice of psychotherapy itself for a deeper treatment in the next section.

(1) Somatic-oriented practices such as yoga, therapeutic massage, acupuncture, Reiki, custom-built exercise, and dance, voice, and musical instrument training all center our consciousness in our bodies and teach us how to balance, rebalance, and invigorate them. (2) Meditation and centering prayer help us build our focus and observation "muscles" such that we become experts at activating the parasympathetic nervous system and its "relaxation response". Then we can increasingly experience what comes into our minds without becoming beholden to, or getting stuck in, any one piece of it.

(3) Studying masterpieces of the mythopoetic mind such as, for example, the parables of God-filled Jesus of Nazareth, the poems of the thirteenth century Sufi mystic Rumi, the existential philosophy of Israeli philosopher Martin Buber (1878-1965), and/or the mind-expanding findings of mythologist Joseph Campbell opens us to an invigorating experience of ourselves as an integral part of a huge earth and cosmic consciousness. (4) Spontaneous writing can reveal to us what needs to be attended to inside of ourselves and sometimes even suggest how to proceed.

(5) Creatively imagining our ideal inner and outer worlds, maybe in conjunction with a hypnotic induction, can give us the concentrated and focused energy to broaden and actualize heretofore untapped potentials. (6) Working with personality classification systems such as the Enneagram or the Myers-Briggs Type Indicator can help us better understand both our natural gifts and our most likely blinds-spots.

(7) Reaching out to our fellow human beings who have

fallen on hard times with a shared laugh and a helping hand can immediately refresh the souls of both the receiver and the giver. (8) Making regular and loving connections with nature and its creatures leads us to our natural biophilia and reminds us that at the deepest level we humans are absolutely a part of nature rather than its master.

(9) Connecting with the arts such as in streaming music, listening to the recordings of our record or CD collections, attending musical concerts, or visiting art gallery exhibits—or traveling "in pilgrimage" to stimulating sites afar—ignites our innate appreciation of beauty, adventure and our fellow human creators. Beyond this, actually creating art, ourselves, puts us in touch with both the power of our own earthly bodies and the ethereal "music of the spheres."

(10) And, finally, study of our nighttime dreams can give us great insight as to where we are in our lives at the current moment. Dreams are sleep-time emanations from the natural self that underlies our culturally created tales of who we are and what we are about. While they are sometimes blurry or non-linear and thus can be confusing—even from time to time horrifying or embarrassing—they are often a great source of vital data about who we are in the deepest sense and even about how we might best proceed in our lives.

I had a beautiful dream when I was a therapy client in my late twenties. I appeared in it as a very young boy walking hand in hand with my parents as we made our way through desert sands touring the grand monuments of ancient Egypt. As we proceeded past the Great Pyramid, I noticed a long-forgotten stone staircase ascending up its backside. Without hesitation, I broke free of my parents' hands and ran to the stairs and climbed them, clearing debris of the centuries to make my way. When I reached the top, I looked out at a rolling, verdant Eden. I was immediately aware that all of the inhabitants of this magical land were treated equally and buried when they died without fuss or fanfare. This dream has been my call to individuation ever since the night I had it over forty years ago.

Let me offer a few thoughts that might help you become (more) interested and adept in exploring your dreams. First, could you assume that rather than trying to disguise things and confuse you, your inner dream-maker is actually speaking to you in a language of images that is the "elder sibling" of our language of words? Could you open yourself to the possibility that your dreams are acts of inner-rebalancing that automatically provide you with a healing touch whether or not you remember them and work with them for further insight?

And could you approach a dream that interests you with these simple first questions: "What aspect of me or my consciousness does this dream highlight?" And then, maybe, "Why might this aspect of how I think and/or feel be presenting itself to me right now?" And then, also, "Can I enter into an imaginative conversation with any especially potent or dynamic object or character of my dream?"

QUESTIONS FOR THE READER

Could you get into a practice of thanking your awesome dream-maker for their offerings, thus developing an ongoing relationship with them as you would with a dear friend?

Which of the self-healing modes listed above most light you up? Why do you think this is?

Do you remember one of your nighttime dreams that either confuses or inspires you? Could you put into words what you think it might be saying to you?

CHAPTER SEVEN
WORDS FOR CONTEMPLATION I

QUESTION #7

What do psychological thinkers and psychotherapists whom you admire have to say about psychological growth?

ANSWER #7

Following are thoughts of some of my favorite professional and personal associates, as well as authors whom I've "befriended" over the years. Hopefully several will touch you deeply. If you have an emotional response to a particular offering, take time to reflect on it. It might very well lead you into the magical world of YOUR OWN ecstasy and wisdom.

I have arranged the contributions into "wisdom sets" of two or three quotes. I suggest that you think of them as ongoing conversations among the contributors. Join where you feel intrigued. And join only as many conversations at a sitting as you wish. Feel free at any time to move forward to the next section of the book, "How About Psychotherapy?" that begins with Question #8, to come back later to the remainder of the quotes.

(The inclusion of a contributor's name and words here does not necessarily mean that they endorse all of my ideas or those of the others who are quoted.)

"I only know what everyone else knows in their bones: That life is a journey. That the journey has distinct stages we call childhood, adolescence, adulthood, and elderhood. That every stage of life has its distinct purpose and beauty – even those like adolescence and old age which we as a culture seem to trash."

— David Oldfield (contemporary)

"Life is a series of natural and spontaneous changes. Don't resist them—that only creates sorrow."

— Lao Tzu (circa 6th c. B.C.E.)

"If I live to be old enough, I may sit down under some bush, the last left in the utilitarian world, and feel thankful that intellect in its march has spared one vestige of the ancient forest for me to die by."

— Thomas Cole (1801-1848)

"I have found that I need lots of tools in my toolbox to get through difficult times. The tools that work best for me involve focusing.

My go-tos are walking, breathing, and getting good sleep. Cooking has also been a constant for me, and with that, feeding people. And chocolate-making. The beauty of chocolate-making is that it takes your full attention; one must watch temperatures, times, environmental conditions, ingredients...but it lends itself to endless variation and creativity."

— Martha Young (contemporary)

"Let's face it, a nice creamy chocolate cake does a lot for a lot of people. It does me."

— Audrey Hepburn (1929-1993)

←————————————————→

"With practice, we can see that our wounded child is not only us... Our mother may have suffered throughout her life. Our father may have suffered. So when we're embracing the wounded child in us, we are embracing all wounded children... in the numberless generations of ancestors and descendents."

—Thich Nhat Hanh (1926-2022)

"At the passing of my teacher Thich Nhat Hanh I am reminded that no one can escape the death gate. We all must go through it sooner or later. Hopefully we will be prepared and happy to leave when our turn comes."

— Bernard Schultz (contemporary)

47

"I am an artist who serves as a guide for visitors to a renowned contemporary art museum. What I do is help visitors see that they are engaging with something that is made by a human being and that they, as a fellow human being, have an elemental connection, regardless of the rest of their stories and experiences. Forget what you think you should be experiencing or knowing. There is no pedestal, even if there is a physical pedestal that the work is on. Cultivate open awareness."

— Colleen Garibaldi (contemporary)

"A newborn baby has the infinite in its eyes."

— Vincent Van Gogh (1853-1890)

"One day, one moment, I looked up and saw the eyes of my kindergarten teacher seeing me. I saw her see me. There was no assessment, no agenda. She saw me where I was and met me there. Her seeing entered me and took root, engendering a relationship to the Self that has been a growing and ripening thing for more than sixty-four years. Her name was Mrs. Hess."

— Barbara Nance (contemporary)

"Our 67 year marriage has thrived because of our unconditional love for each other. Also because we have worked hard, played even harder, and adored our mother-in-laws and the in-law families.

— Jack and Clarice Fawcett (contemporaries)

"*Emotional intelligence matters twice as much as technical and analytic skill…*"

— Daniel Goleman (contemporary)

"*A simple awareness sustains me, a recognition of the intimate relationship between life and death. From that flows gratitude, compassion, and connection to the living and the dead, human and non-human.*"

— Susan (Elli) Elliott (contemporary)

"*At the level of personality we try to control our life, to determine the course by what we judge as favorable to us. At the level of Self, control gives way to a surrender to what life brings us. The Self-realizing individual is open.*"

— Pierro Ferrucci (contemporary)

"*You wait. Don't be rushed. Hold firm when you know you're right. Redirect if there is something you can't change.*"

— Libby Gardner (contemporary)

"*The relaxation response is a physical state of deep rest that changes the physical and emotional responses to stress… and the opposite of the fight or flight response.*"

— Herbert Benson (contemporary)

"We cannot safely assume that other people's minds work on the same principles as our own. All too often, others with whom we come in contact do not reason as we reason, or do not value the things we value, or are not interested in what interests us."

— Isabel Briggs Myers (1897-1980)

"Young people are not necessarily modern, and old people are not necessarily pre-modern. The difference is not in age but in consciousness and the related lifestyle."

— Henri Nouwen (1932-1966)

"As many observers before me have noticed, humans suffer more in anticipation and in their minds than is necessary or 'in their flesh.'"

— Carlos Picone (contemporary)

"The greatest and most important problems in life can never be solved, but only outgrown, resulting in a new level of consciousness. Some higher or wider interest appears on the patient's horizon and through this broadening of his outlook the insoluble problem lose(s) its urgency."

— Carl Jung (1865-1961)

"The dream seems to steer the ego consciousness into an adapted, wise attitude toward life."

— Marie Louise von Frank (1915-1998)

"Dream is the personalized myth, myth the depersonalized dream; both myth and dream are symbolic in the same general way of the dynamics of the psyche."

— Joseph Campbell (1904-1987)

"I remember standing in front of the Mona Lisa. I was mesmerized. I know that some experts think of it as the most beautiful painting in the world. It's not only the visual. It's the emotion that it brings up."

— Evelyn Story (contemporary)

"It is not what the dream image is about; it's what field of energy it is activating."

— James Hollis (contemporary)

"I help clients see two specific things: (1.) What we say and do can influence others, but the only person we control is ourselves; and (2.) True equality among ethnicities, genders, and religious groups comes from our learning to respect others and treating them as we wish to be treated."

— Suzan Stafford (contemporary)

"My long and beautiful life has had everything to do with my father Vitale Vitale. He escaped the horrors in Italy under Mussolini, and brought us, his family, with him to New York. We had a very loving family."

— Rita DeLuise (contemporary)

"Everything can be taken from a man but one thing: the last of the human freedoms—to choose one's attitude—one's own way."

— Victor Frankl (1905-1997)

"I've learned that wisdom comes from having an open heart and an open mind."

— Frances Nance (contemporary)

"People are just as wonderful as sunsets if you let them be...I don't try to control sunset. I watch with awe as it unfolds."

— Carl Rogers (1902-1987)

"Since I was a kid, walking has been the number one way I sort out problems. Often it takes days or weeks. And of course the exercise factor is huge. As an adult, for more than forty years now, music is almost as important as walking. When my mind is in a loop, I listen to music to break the cycle."

— Judith Lorimer (contemporary)

"I've trekked through Myanmar, Ethiopia, and Tibet to try to help myself understand the ways that other people solve the problem of how to raise families satisfactorily, and how to help with the injustice in the world."

— Jeanne Waples (contemporary)

"The life abroad in Indonesia that Wes, Blaine, and I undertook was deepened and sweetened by the calmness, grace, and kindness of our mentor Pak Suwito. He personified the Indonesian national slogan "Unity in Diversity".

— Mary Jo Gibson

"I'll never forget our night in remote Kerambitan on the south coast of Bali. We were awakened by the sound of gamelan music in the distance. We found our way through the dark to a group of old and young men — farmers from the surrounding rice fields — playing their instruments in the temple under a single bare light bulb. They invited us to sit with them. The full moon rose."

— Mitchell Story

←———————————→

"I reached out to my neighbor Diane (aka Pooh Bear), and she graciously reached back. Despite our different races and very different histories, we quickly became friends. Together, we accomplish projects for the common good in the neighborhood. Our wonderful bond confirms my belief that we humans are all at our cores the same."

— Patti Fleck (contemporary)

"Our lively and high spirited mum Rosina moved through difficult situations such as breaking her hip and having to learn how to walk again amazingly well. It was because of her never-wavering positivity and her super strong will."

— Emiliana Garbo (contemporary)

←———————————→

"I've been a recording engineer for five decades, mostly at Nola Studios in Manhattan. I've observed that the greatest musicians are great listeners. They are receptive to everything going on in the room. In live performances, they really hear — and respond to — the feelings of their audience."

— John Post (contemporary)

"I still believe in goodness; I still believe in love. I know the power of a healing touch when the going gets rough. If I choose to harden my heart, I'm nothing at all."

— Laura Love (contemporary)

"Treasure the past—the familiarity and affirmation of community in it—but the future holds newness and adventure! Sharing the past with new people is important; creating new memories with them is the goal. Be bold!"

— Betsy Scanlin (contemporary)

"Some phrases I don't like are: 'baby steps', 'I'm not ready', 'I'm trying', 'That's outside my comfort zone', these thoughts are impotent, baby steps are for babies. Life happens when you challenge yourself, push yourself forward, do those things you think you can't. When you step outside your comfort zone and linger, your comfort zone will expand to meet you."

— Thomas Gaebel (contemporary)

"I want to say, I believe very much in dialogue. And I really believe that we can recreate the world by acting courageously. To act with courage is to have concrete hope in a better future.

We carve out a small space of the world. We shape and reshape it and in that way, small slice by small slice, we work slowly, yes, but we walk on the path of real progress.

Courage and hope are intertwined. Courage is an act of hope and hope is born of courage. Acts of courage create hope and there is nothing more essential to the human spirit than hope. So, here's to courage."

— Chimamanda Ngozi Adichie (contemporary)

PART TWO

HOW ABOUT PSYCHOTHERAPY?

A. First Thoughts

CHAPTER EIGHT
PSYCHOTHERAPY

QUESTION #8

What is psychotherapy?

ANSWER #8

When our self-care measures are not stemming the tide of our inner or outer problems—or when we need to do major problem solving about which fork in the road of our lives to take and which to leave behind—reaching out to a professional psychotherapist might be something to consider.

Psychotherapy, sometimes simply called "therapy" or "personal counseling," is an encounter between a person who seeks help with emotional or behavioral difficulties and a person who has expertise in such matters and uses it to guide the client to their best self.

Since there are a number of ideas about what most helps clients, there are several kinds of psychotherapy. And since psychotherapists have different professional identifications, the person with expertise you seek out may be called a psychologist, a clinical social worker, a psychiatrist, a personal counselor, a nurse, a pastoral counselor, or something else. We will look into these particulars in the next Question and Answer.

But for starters, the term "psychotherapy" literally means "healing the soul." I like to think of us humans as soul-creatures who have all sorts of sensitivities and potentials that arise from our formidable bodies and our complex, unique brains and nervous systems. With this complexity comes complication. Mood-wise, our natural joy in living can turn into an anxiety about our lives, a sense of melancholy, a frustrated anger. Behaviorally, our propensity to accomplish goals both big and small and to enjoy the beauty and mysteries that surround us can devolve into obsessive behavior, addictive behavior, or inertia.

Psychotherapy tunes into our deep human need to be heard and nurtured in a caring relationship. It uses this relationship to help us heal ourselves. At best, the therapy relationship can, over time, provide us with a sturdier sense of self for making spontaneous, healthy connections to ourselves and to our world.

QUESTIONS FOR THE READER

Do you think that doing some psychotherapy would make sense for you?

If you are already in therapy, is it helping you? What would make it better or more productive?

CHAPTER NINE
FINDING A THERAPIST

QUESTION #9

You mentioned that there are different kinds of therapists and therapy. If I decide to engage a therapist, how could I ever know who would best understand me and help me?

ANSWER #9

In observing many different therapists over the years, I have come to believe that compassion, empathy, intelligence, and experience, rather than any particular professional identification such as "psychiatrist," "psychologist," "social worker," "personal counselor," or "analyst" are—bottom line—what makes a therapist excellent at their work.

If a trusted family member, friend, or colleague can recommend a therapist from any of the various professions with whom they have had a good experience, that would be a lead. Also, you can go to the Internet and find recommendations at "psychotherapist near me," Psychology Today, or the websites of professional organizations such as the D.C. Psychological Association or various state associations.

If you receive a recommendation that seems viable, call, e-mail, or text and get a sense of your prospective therapist through the rhythm and content of the conversation that ensues. Pay attention to whether the therapist seems to want to get a feel for your particular situation, or if they seem more interested in selling a point of view or method. Notice, too, if the therapist is clear about policies, procedures, and fee without making them the central point of the conversation. If the therapist exhibits a gentle humor, that is a real plus, because intelligent humor is often a good icebreaker at the beginning of therapy and helpful throughout the entire process.

When talking to your potential therapist, you might hear a reference to the type of therapy to which they subscribe. "Psychodynamic," "cognitive-behavioral," "mind-body," "analytic," "grief," "family systems," "trauma," "gestalt," "eclectic" and many other labels are descriptors of a therapist's expertise, point of view, and/or treatment method. Pay some attention to these, and if you don't know what they mean, be sure to ask.

Someone who needs medication to tamp down or rev up extreme emotions would at least initially best work with a psychiatrist, a medical doctor who is an expert in what we call "psychopharmacological medications" such as anti-depressants and anti-anxiety drugs.

Those who are usually more even-keeled in mood or

temperament but are having a hard time with the loss of an important-other in a breakup or a death might see a grief therapist. Someone who thinks they might have an addiction to alcohol, drugs, or pornography would best seek out an addiction counselor. Someone who has experienced deeply hurtful emotional wounding might see a trauma specialist.

Psychodynamic therapists and cognitive behavioral (CBT) therapists help us explore and work through troubling and unproductive aspects of our inner and outer worlds such that we can live more robustly and joyfully. Psychodynamic therapists emphasize the historical and unconscious aspects of the client's life and attempt to make meaningful bridges and connections from there to the client's current life, while cognitive-behavioral therapists work with the client's core beliefs and resulting behaviors.

Some therapists draw from an array of these traditions and points of view and call themselves "eclectic." And truth be told, even therapists who are known for a particular specialty might actually be knowledgeable in other areas or techniques as well.

But here's what I'd recommend that you do even before making a contact with a potential therapist: have an interview with yourself! Based on your answers, you can tell the professional you interview about YOU, an ask if they are appropriately trained and feel comfortable in working with a person with your profile.

Here are some self-interview questions:

— *Why am I thinking about engaging a therapist AT THIS TIME?*

— *Do I have some kind of deep grief or trauma in my background? If so, how am I coping?*

— *Have I ever done therapy before? If so, did it work out for me?*

— *Am I in an emotional emergency?*

— *Do I have a secret to tell?*

— *What would I like to learn or gain from therapy?*

— *Do I have any fears about the therapeutic process?*

— *Do I seek a few sessions, or longer work?*

— *For a therapist to really "get me," what would they most need to know about me?*

    (Make this succinct so that you can state it in a sentence or two.)

While you might not be able to answer all of these questions immediately, engaging in a process of reflection on what you do know about your hopes and expectations will help you eventually express yourself in your interview or interviews with possible helpers.

If you choose to move forward, I hope that you find a wonderful therapist guide. I hope that you find someone akin to one of the two clinicians I embrace in memory in this book's dedication above. They are my own long-term therapist, Harold Lindner, and my dear friend and colleague, Louise de Leeuw. These amazing individuals each conveyed an unwavering belief in the worth of every individual with whom they worked. In addition, Hal had the gift of audacity: "Why not?" was his question. And Louise had the gifts of a huge heart and a commitment to forward movement: "I see, I understand,"— and then, after a long Quaker pause —"and now how do we make progress on this?" was her refrain.

QUESTIONS FOR THE READER

If you are considering doing some therapy, what are the first, unguarded words out of your mouth or from your pen about why you think you need it or want it, and what you hope to get out of it? What therapist's style do you think would best fit you?

CHAPTER TEN
GENDER AND LGBTQ ISSUES

QUESTION #10

I have heard that psychotherapy is a mostly a female-oriented activity. Is there a place for men in therapy?

And how about LGBTQ people? I know that gay and transgender people have sometimes been pathologized by the psychological establishment.

ANSWER #10

My own therapists, supervisors, colleagues, and supervisees over the years have been a wonderful mix of women and men, straight and gay. My clients also, with a tilt toward men. But I have read credible accounts that men in the U.S—and in fact around the world—are half as likely as women to seek out therapy. So where is the disconnect between men and psychotherapy coming from?

We know that there are gender-based brain differences that can push young male and female focus and status-seeking strategies in different directions from our earliest days. Typical little girls, so it seems, have strong tendencies to prioritize emotional communication, while typical little boys are more drawn to mastering objects. A notion that evolves from this research is that interpersonal communication and connection—the bread and butter of psychotherapy—are not in the wheelhouse of the "average" boy and man, and, consequently, that psychotherapy and men do not make much of a match.

But let's not forget the power of human individuality and how it often overrules gender stereotypes. Some men are, in fact, quite good at experiencing and expressing their deep emotions and enjoy doing so. And many men who are interpersonally or intimately challenged can grow their emotional awareness and expression skills with good individual, group, and/or couples therapy.

Movie actor and director Ben Affleck (contemporary) is reflective about his boyhood and his less than perfect early relationship with his father. In a 2021 interview with Wall Street journal writer Michael Hainey, he states that, "Most boys want their fathers to be heroes. They want to learn about what is expected to become a man." When fathering is imperfect, he continues, an emotional fallout for the boy is often shame, which is "corrosive."

I believe that Affleck highlights what leads a good number of men to enter therapy, whatever their presenting symptom or problem. These clients consciously or unconsciously seek to break out of the shame that an absent, abusive, or insensitive father, mother, and/or culture has visited upon them. Their therapeutic work involves throwing off some of the emotional armor built up around their vulnerabilities, so as to experience and internalize an authentic, non-shame-based connection with the therapist. Hopefully, the client then integrates this type of interaction into more of his ongoing relationships in the world.

Some men in therapy then go on to identify and pursue a personal "hero's journey." In this work, the client—like the heroes of ancient myth—begins to explore heretofore avoided inner or outer frontiers with the goal of bringing back a boon of new understanding and experience for his own good and the good of others he cares about.

The LGBTQ community was indeed pathologized by some of the early twentieth century founders of psychotherapy and others who followed them. It wasn't until 1973 — after a number of heated verbal exchanges between psychiatrists of differing persuasions at regional and national gatherings, as well as a number of physical clashes between pro-gay demonstrators and crowd control police commencing with New York City's 1969 Stonewall riots—that the American Psychiatric Association took homosexuality off its list of mental disorders. But even since that date, LGBTQ therapists are still seen in certain quarters as insufficiently whole to be helping others, and LGBTQ clients are still viewed in those same quarters as deficient in mental health BECAUSE OF

69

their sexual orientation.

At its worst, members of ultra-conservative religious-therapeutic communities continue to promote what they call "conversion therapy" or "reparative therapy" which has the goal of changing a client's homosexual orientation into a heterosexual one. We have come to know that this does not work as advertised, and that it, in fact, can plunge people into anxiety, depression, self-hatred and—in the most tragic cases—suicide. Thankfully, the accepted notion in mainstream psychotherapy circles today is that therapists should affirm LGBTQ clients' initiatives to live lives congruent with their natures.

There have always been excellent LGBTQ therapists. In the early days of psychotherapy, they generally kept their orientations hidden so as to be able to practice in peace. Since the mid-1970's, many, myself included, practice openly. Some LGBTQ therapists actually advertise their sexual or gender orientations to signal LGBTQ clients that they will be received affirmatively in their practices.

Some of us gay therapists have been inspired by a traditional belief of a number of Native American communities that "two-spirited" people—folks with a certain "in-betweenness" status—can be especially good communicators and healers. Maybe my own two-spirited side was coming through in a session one day many years ago when a straight male client struggling with how to rise above his difficult youth trusted our connection enough to indulge a hunch and ask me if I am gay. When I confirmed his guess, he paused. After several long seconds, he looked up, met my gaze, and said, "Well, okay, now I know that you've suffered too." Our connection deepened. Our work intensified.

QUESTIONS FOR THE READER

If you are a male person, or an LGBTQ person, and are considering doing therapy, what would you hope that your therapist would come to know about your personality and your history to best help you?

What would you hope that psychotherapy could offer you?

B. The Client Experience

CHAPTER ELEVEN
SHORT AND ONGOING THERAPY

QUESTION #11

What are short-term therapy and ongoing therapy?

ANSWER #11

Short-term therapy seeks to address a client need that is specific and usually behavioral. Short-term therapy goals are definable and limited in number. Examples would be a twelve-session course of work to learn assertiveness techniques, keep anxious thoughts under control, learn how to better nurture a child with ADHD, or initiate a smoking-cessation program.

In ongoing or long-term therapy, the client and therapist establish a relationship for an extended period of time that might not only relieve an immediate symptom, but will also hopefully change the climate of the client's inner world and expand their range of behaviors in their outer world. The highest goal of ongoing therapy is that the client will end up having access to more of their whole self and thus lean toward greater optimism and resilience.

Ongoing therapy often has a more or less predictable arc. In the initial stage, the client and therapist get to know each other. The client shares their concerns and history while the therapist extends empathic listening and intelligently timed questions and suggestions. The therapist and client commit to working through any occurrences in the therapy itself that are confusing and/or painful to the client.

As the therapy progresses to its middle phase, the client's more hidden or projected fears and passions are identified and explored. Also, the character and tone of the client-therapist partnership becomes more and more internalized by the client, and they begin to use it to deal with the difficult issues of their life in the world. This middle phase has its bursts of progress and its retreats and can last for a relatively short period of time or for a number of years, depending on the severity of the client's issues and their appetite for self-examination and taking new actions in the world.

At some point, the client's desire to return to a life without formal help asserts itself, and the final phase of therapy ensues. It involves a summing up of what will be important to remember through the years after therapy, or maybe for the years after this particular round of therapy. The highest expression of the kind of deep growth that can occur in long-term therapy is a client's gratitude for having been given their own particular human life and a commitment to live it fully.

Many kinds of "soul issues," as well as many issues of life

in the world, bring clients into ongoing therapy. But two that are consistently represented are trauma and grief.

Trauma and its possible aftermath of "post traumatic stress" arise when a person experiences a noxious and/ or terrifying situation against their own will and with little possibility of escape or getting help. Examples range from a young employee being forced to engage in sex with a boss in order to keep their job; a child being repeatedly bullied on the school playground; or soldiers living through a battle in which they are physically and/or emotionally wounded.

Trauma often leaves its victims with excruciating emotions such as rage, shame, and fear. In the worst kinds of cases, it can even negatively alter a person's optimal brain development and full genetic expression. Traumatized people can experience an understandable tendency to split off their horrible experiences from the rest of themselves, while concurrently, in the words of trauma expert Dr. Bessel van der Kolk, "becoming living testimonials for things that no longer exist."

My colleague Dr. Richard Boesch tells us that, "trauma becomes a part of us that lives in our body and remains out of place, continuing to cause us pain." In ongoing therapy, he continues, the client and their therapist, "touch it gently at first, massage it through our own special ways of talking about it, and help it find a place inside of us where it belongs."

My colleague Dr. Jean Gearon explains that, "when a client

shares the deep shame they live with as a result of trauma, I ask them to help me understand what they have experienced more deeply. They cannot deepen my understanding without deepening their own. It is in this breath of a moment, that the isolation demanded by the shame and trauma begins to soften its grip."

Because we humans bond with those we have and those we love, we all experience loss and grief when life shifts and changes. Sometimes because of the severity of a loss, such as in losing one's child, spouse, parent, health, valued career, country, or cherished pet, grief can feel overwhelming.

When, almost forty years ago now, our father died alone in a hospital room between our mother's evening visit and her planned visit for the next morning, I wrote, "All of Dad and Mom's hopes and dreams together just ended in silence, without a shared whisper of 'goodbye.' How could this be?" I remembered back to how cozy I had felt as a tiny child when Dad held me in his lap and read to me; I recalled his habit of getting up in the middle of the night and worrying over things—changing his rings from one finger to another so as to alert himself the next morning to the insights he had gained during the night. Several days later, when I looked at Dad laid out in his coffin, I gazed at his face. His *Italian-ness* emerged for me. I thought of the alternative lives that this face suggested: a New York City stock exchange broker, perhaps; or even a benevolent Renaissance prince. And then, returning,

I saw my beautiful dad as he now was. There was no time left for us.

My colleague Dr. Elizabeth Haase talks about the amelioration of deep grief in ongoing therapy: "No one can ever really understand the unique grief of another person. But we as therapists can stand beside the grieving client, providing ballast in the stormy days, weeks, months, and years as our clients learn to live in a world without the one to whom they were so attached either in love, or in other significant ways."

QUESTIONS FOR THE READER

If you are thinking about doing therapy, which of the two therapy models—short-term or ongoing—seems like it would probably best fit your needs? If you already in therapy, is it meeting your needs?

CHAPTER TWELVE

DOES THERAPY FOR ONE PERSON REALLY MATTER?

QUESTION #12

In the face of global turmoil and deprivation, does psychotherapy for single individuals really make any sense or any difference? Also, should therapists who spend most of their time seeing individual clients be reaching out beyond their consulting rooms?

ANSWER #12

It is absolutely true that navel-gazing in therapy while the world falls apart around us would be selfish and counterproductive. It would be akin to getting completely caught up in a dopamine-hit-inducing video game and failing to notice that our home is burning down around us.

Psychotherapy is about hope. In enlightened therapy, rays of hope stream in two different directions. First, they stream toward the client, the individual who over time ameliorates their pain and broadens their perspective. But secondly, they stream out from the client to the world. Martin Luther King

Jr. gives us the underlying dynamic. "Whatever affects one directly, affects all indirectly."

The American psychiatrist-writer Irvin Yalom (contemporary), speaking of himself and of his fellow psychotherapists, states, "We take pleasure not only in the growth of the patient but also in the ripple effect—the salutary influence our patients have upon those whom they touch in life."

My home professional organization, the DC Psychological Association, reminds us Washington, D.C. therapists in private practices to devote some of our time and expertise to helping people beyond those who normally seek us out and pay our standard fees, and to develop the cultural competence to work well with these folks.

Providing one or several members of underserved communities with ongoing therapy for a reduced fee or no fee at all, and/or facilitating support groups for vulnerable people such as immigrants recently arrived to our country, are examples of worthy outreaches.

My DCPA colleague Dr. Laurie Paul conducts and reviews research with an eye to helping us better understand diverse populations, and bend our sensibilities toward social justice. In her review of research on race relations in our country, she finds that, "most black Americans can see through our (Caucasian) unconscious defenses around race and may see bias in us that we don't even see ourselves." To me, this finding turns the tables for a moment on us white therapists as the "givers," and focuses us rather on how we might "receive" valuable insights about ourselves from clients (and therapists) of other races, while still, of course, always keeping our therapeutic focus on the goal of helping the unique person at hand in whatever ways they might need our help.

QUESTIONS FOR THE READER

Do you imagine that doing some therapy might lead you to become more hopeful, not only for yourself, but also for the world? ?

If you are a therapist, are you reaching out to any individual or individuals who could benefit from your services but need(s) to be seen on a pro-bono basis? Are you doing any work with underprivileged communities?

CHAPTER THIRTEEN

GROUP AND COUPLES THERAPY

QUESTION #13

Why do some therapy clients choose to do group sessions or couples sessions rather than individual sessions?

ANSWER #13

May I tell you a very old story out of India? One day the Buddha came upon a young woman who had lost her infant son to death. She clutched the baby's body to her breast. Fellow villagers could not console her. Gautama Siddhartha put a hand on the deceased baby's head. He then turned to the mother and asked if she could call up the energy to bring him a handful of mustard seeds from a house in the village whose family had never lost a member to death. She agreed, maybe thinking that the Buddha would eventually prepare a tonic with the collected seeds that would bring her baby back to life. As she made her way from one abode to the next and began to realize that no family has ever been spared death, her panic began to subside. She returned to the Buddha and laid her baby's body down to rest.

This ancient tale of compassion illustrates one of the deepest healing possibilities available to us when we open ourselves to our fellow human beings. We begin to realize that other people experience suffering similar to our own, and therein we are encouraged to keep going. A wide variety of people are helped by circles of folks who are sensitive to their unique histories and needs. Twelve-step groups such as Alcoholics Anonymous, or support groups for people going though any number of different illnesses or grief, are great examples. Group Therapy—a circle of six to eight members in groups that I facilitate—provides members with a forum for working through both internal blocks and inter-personal issues.

I facilitate a gay men's therapy group, and I recently asked members what the greatest benefit of participating in our group has been for each of them. I got several answers. One member told me that group therapy gives him the opportunity to both get and give advice. He is referencing what I call the group "problem-solving benefit." This factor can feel like leaning over the back fence to get an opinion from a smart neighbor and then getting opinions from not just one but seven intelligent parties.

Another of our members mentioned that he values belonging to an embracing peer group. A group therapy circle can be an affirming and encouraging home that may actually be more validating than some members' childhood families or even current friendship circles. I always try to promote the tone of a loving family in the group circle such that members feel both accepted for who they are and challenged to become their best selves.

Thoughtful group therapy participants note that this type of interaction works best for them when they think of it as an ongoing practice, similar maybe to doing yoga or meditation in community. The benefit is usually experienced not by what happens during a single session, but rather in the continuing refining of both problems and resolutions in the ongoing interactions amongst the members.

Couples Therapy is sessions for two people together, usually two personal partners. Folks often seek out this kind of therapy when they are having trouble communicating effectively with each other. A deeper wound that brings in some pairs is a loss of trust in each other.

"Couples Work 101" is learning or re-learning empathic listening. This involves slowing down conversations such that each important thought or feeling of each party is expressed and understood before going on to the next.

It might seem surprising, but two people who live together as a couple may not really hear and/or understand each other's most important thoughts and feelings very well. Misunderstandings may revolve around concrete aspects of life such as money management, dealing with difficult in-laws, or sharing home maintenance tasks. They can also arise from more soul and spirit oriented things such as how to think about religion in child rearing, how to make a healing environment for a partner's addiction recovery, how to deal with the serious illness or impending death of one of the partners or their parents, or how to have a more mutually satisfying sex life.

An even deeper challenge that some partners take on in couple's therapy is looking squarely at the dynamics of their relationship itself. In the early "limerence phase of romance," we often feel quite deeply but see only vaguely. Now the task is to uncover the often less-than-fully-conscious fantasies and hopes each member had for choosing the other, see how these have been fulfilled and inevitably disappointed since that early glow, and adjust to the reality of who each other really is in current life. When this happens, new hope for the relationship and even new joy can sometimes emerge.

Some deeply troubled couples, though, eventually come to the conclusion that the gap between what they want and what they have is too much to bridge, and they decide to break up. In these cases, final sessions can be about the terms of disengagement, hopefully without having to demonize the other or place too heavy a guilt on oneself.

A delightful kind of couples work ensues when I get a call from an excited person who tells me that she and her beau, for instance, are planning marriage and want to sit down and talk with a therapist to make sure that they are committing with their eyes wide open. In these sessions, the consulting room is filled with hope. The couple can talk about how grateful they are for each other as well as explore the shadows in their connection. They might even be willing to contemplate how their relationship can lead each of them to be a more engaged person in the broader world, maybe as a parent, maybe as a better friend and citizen.

QUESTIONS FOR THE READER

If you were to choose to do some therapy (or more), which mode do you think would be most helpful to you—individual, group, or couples work? Why?

C. Therapists

CHAPTER FOURTEEN
QUALITIES OF GOOD THERAPISTS

QUESTION #14

In your opinion, what characteristics should a person have, or cultivate, in order to become a good therapist?

ANSWER #14

Good therapists, like good mediators, must first and foremost be able to sit. They need to be able to give their focused attention to another person for an hour or so many times over on a busy day.

A good therapist should be a person of compassion, someone who can feel tenderly toward folks in distress. That compassion, combined with an ability to see into the "perceived world" of another person while at the same time remaining true to one's own real self, is the coin of the realm in psychotherapy. When clients come to know that we are giving both our empathy and our genuineness freely and consistently, they often move toward claiming their own wholeness in the sessions and in their lives.

A good therapist needs to develop discernment. This starts with what psychotherapy pioneer Melanie Klein (1882-1960) refers to as learning how "to pick out the point of urgency" in a client's presenting situation. It also involves becoming familiar with the diagnostic and treatment language of the mental health world (DSM-5-TR, ICD, and CPT diagnoses and codes, for instance) and how its terms apply to our clients.

Former NIMH Director Thomas Insel MD and others remind us that a good therapist should understand that, while formal diagnoses can educate us about clusters of symptoms that often appear together in certain individuals, they do not define the identity of any one of the unique people who become our therapy clients. Our treatment strategies should be developed not only on the basis of formal diagnoses, but also on the basis of best practice norms, our own philosophical orientations, and—most importantly— on our understandings and intuitions that arise out of the relationships that we form with the individuals whom we seek to help.

And, very importantly, good therapists should think and act ethically. First and foremost, acting ethically entails treating our clients with the same respect and attention that we would a family member or a good friend. In addition, we need to study and follow the special ethical codes of our professions. Each of these includes such basic principles as "informed consent" (the client and therapist should both know and agree on the nature of the therapy), "confidentiality" (with a few very specific exceptions, the therapist should hold and safeguard what the client reveals in sessions), and "correct boundaries" (the therapist should not get involved with the client in any way that violates the therapeutic nature of the relationship.)

There are always young "old souls" in our midst, but I believe that for most of us, having some personal experience of the joys and sorrows of adult life before beginning work as a therapist is helpful. I think of how the future Buddha began understanding human suffering only after he escaped his kingly father's closed compound and encountered an old man, a sick man, a dead man, and a wanderer.

Ongoing learning is a great boon for us therapists. Continuing study keeps us alert, spontaneous, and in "beginner's mind," the opposite of thinking, "I know it all." My own ongoing learning over the years has deepened my understanding of the very distinct types of communications that occur between our clients and ourselves in our sessions. While therapeutic dialogue can sometimes be a straightforward give and take between two problem-solving adults, it can also include emotional projections on the part of the client, the therapist, or both. And, in an even more complicated turn, it might also include client communications that are unconsciously meant to invoke in the therapist the difficult feelings that they carry in their lives. I have come to know that the more we anticipate, understand, and work with these various types of communications, the greater chance we have of mining the whole range of healing possibilities for our clients.

More broadly, our ongoing education programs can cue us in to startling discoveries that are being made on the frontiers of psychological learning. Neurobiologists, for instance, are unearthing the heretofore undreamed of plasticity of the human brain; they are showing us that brain health and higher states of consciousness can evolve even into our late years. Diversity theorists are formulating ever more sophisticated "minority stress" and "affirmative therapy" models to make our work with society's perceived "outsiders" more effective and worthwhile to them.

Especially in private practice, where we spend so much time "flying solo" working with our clients from our separate offices or on our separate computers and telephones, we should be ready to refer severely troubled clients and/or clients going through complicated crises to psychopharmacologists and/or to clinic settings with support personnel. Certainly we should always be ready to get supervision from respected peers or a more seasoned practitioner when novel and/or possibly dangerous situations with challenging clients or therapeutic impasses arise in our practices.

And finally, I think that we therapists should engage in some therapy of our own as the client. This provides us with a personal experience of healing with the help of a therapist as well as the practical learning of how it occurs.

I love the concept of the "wounded healer." In identifying as such, we embrace our own shadows and vulnerabilities, as well as our talents and strengths. Thus we come to our work with a familiarity of our doubts and distresses, as well as with a personal confidence in our therapeutic powers.

QUESTIONS FOR THE READER

If you are a practicing therapist or a therapist in training, what do you see as your natural therapeutic gifts?

What are the aspects of good practice that might come to you less naturally and thus need your attention in your program of continuing learning?

CHAPTER FIFTEEN
FEMALE THERAPISTS

QUESTION #15

Why were almost all of the early psychotherapists men? Where were the women? And where are the women now?

ANSWER #15

When Carl Jung's spouse and colleague Emma Rauschenbach Jung (1882-1955) died of metastatic cancer, her pastor paid tribute to her in these words: "Her sense of humor...saw through everything that was inflated or one-sided. She resolved difficulties and tensions. She was able to carry and endure life's burdens. And above all, she knew how to recognize and protect the secrets of others."

There have been many wonderfully inspired women therapists and thinkers like Emma Jung from the very beginnings of psychotherapy who have exhibited their talents in a diverse array of styles and arenas. But the patriarchal world of medicine out of which psychotherapy evolved, and our patriarchal world in general, have often failed to highlight the unique qualities of these women. In the early years of psychotherapy, women were not even admitted to medical school. Women of color had to swim upstream against both sexist and racist barriers.

Courageously breaking past these formidable strictures, the American social worker Virginia Satir (1916-1988) developed a great body of work on family dynamics and is widely seen as a founder of family therapy. Swiss-American psychiatrist Elisabeth Kubler-Ross (1926-2004) observed dying and grieving people with a new eye and developed theories and practices for working with them such that she is esteemed as a great "pioneer of grief therapy."

In our own times, there have been major gender advances in the field. A majority of the currently practicing psychotherapists in the United States who come from psychology and social work traditions are women. Women constitute thirty-some percent of working psychiatrists and over fifty percent of psychiatric residents. Many of these women are leaders in their specialties.

In 2022, the two immediate past presidents, the current president, and the president-elect of the D.C. Psychological Association—Dr. Suzan Stafford, Dr. Victoria Sylos-Labini, Dr. Samira Paul, and Dr. Laurie Paul—are all widely respected female therapists. In the best tradition of female holistic thinking and nurturing, they each in their own way promote a proactive outreach to communities that have been traditionally under-represented in therapy.

The national organization for psychologists, the APA,

awarded its 2022 National Diversity Award to the D.C. Psychological Association. In her gracious acceptance speech, President Samira Paul emphasized the importance of valuing and understanding "the unique context of each (client's) lived experience."

A QUESTION FOR THE READER

What do you imagine the profession of psychotherapy has gained by overcoming its early reluctance to accept women and other minorities into its ranks of psychotherapists?

CHAPTER SIXTEEN
THE FUTURE OF THERAPY

QUESTION #16

Does psychotherapy have a future?

ANSWER #16

Soul-healing has been a deep part of the human endeavor from the beginnings of our days on earth. We engage in it with each other all the time. Therein the loving kiss, the special meal, the perfect gift.

When a particular soul-creature is in unrelenting distress—high or low—a professional tender-of-souls might be engaged. Therein the shaman, the doula, the medicine man. In our times, therein also the psychotherapist.

But in a hundred years, will psychotherapy seem like a quaint idea in the list of humankind's healing endeavors, to be replaced by something new and superior?

Women's advocate, sex therapist, and futurist Dr.

Marianne Brandon writes and lectures on evolving human development. She tells us that practices such as genetically enhancing human fetuses, inserting bolstering microchips in less than optimally functioning human brains, and building robots and avatars that can respond without question and hesitation to our particular needs, are destined to become evermore important elements in our species' attempts to maximize satisfaction and success.

Our question then becomes whether or not the inter-personal intimacy and spontaneity associated with psychotherapy might eventually be replaced by such innovations. My guess is that while new technologies might very well become helpful adjuncts to our work, the therapeutic alliance between the human client and the human therapist will be very difficult, indeed, to replace.

Emotional and spiritual growth seem to develop best in human-to-human relationships of intelligence and regard. When the therapist's genuinely and consistently given empathy meets the client's natural and eternal desire for alignment with their deepest self, the client, I believe, has their best chance for experiencing new energy and growth.

A QUESTION FOR THE READER

Using your intuition and imagination, what would you predict will be the most common issues brought by our great grandchildren to their psychotherapy sessions?

CHAPTER SEVENTEEN
WORDS FOR CONTEMPLATION II

QUESTION #17
What do psychological thinkers whom you admire have to say about psychotherapy and other therapeutic endeavors?

ANSWER #17
(Remember to join only as many conversations at a sitting as you wish. And feel free to move on to Section III and Question #18 when you're ready, returning to remaining discussion rooms later.)

⟵————————⟶

"At a certain point I understood that my therapist was 'bearing witness' to me and that each of us was growing as a human being through our sessions. That liberated something in me. The journey of my life was being shared. And it was sacred. Courage and curiosity and acceptance and joy became available to me in ways I could not have encountered without their witness. It made all the difference."
— Patricia Wudel (contemporary)

"The way the patient perceives the psychotherapist and his relationship with the psychotherapist is the most important factor in therapeutic personality change."

— Ernest Kramer (contemporary)

"Healing is not a linear process. It is a cyclical process. Each of us has a core lesson or two that we are here to learn. We revisit our lessons again and again, each time healing at a deeper level."

— Marilee Aronson (contemporary)

"The future is an infinite succession of presents…"

— Howard Zinn (1922-2010)

"Trauma survivors who spend years dissociating from their memories and their pain sometimes manage to stay connected to their bodies and their hopes through an involvement in the performance arts. My future involves becoming a therapist who helps clients heal through movement and voice."

— Ayanna Blue (contemporary)

"Through the mind-body approaches, a heightened state of consciousness is achieved which leads to increases in cognitive, emotional, and perceptual awareness."

— Stephen Stein (contemporary)

← —————————————————→

"I give each of my patients a rock to hold in their hands. It is to remind them that they have something solid and beautiful beyond their symptoms."

— Geri Zagoric (contemporary)

"Among the gifts I offer patients though acupuncture is the permission to fully experience an array of emotions, both mentally and physically, to identify where emotion sits in their body, and to 'dance' with them in their expansive way. In our culture we offer pills to mask emotions like anger, grief, sadness, fear. In healing with acupuncture, patients can be encouraged to move through these mind and body experiences, never feeling sick, and appreciate how the emotion allowed them to process real life experiences and responses."

— Bronwyn Clark (contemporary)

← —————————————————→

"So much of therapy is about embracing the 'and.' So often we struggle with the one thing and reject it almost immediately with our 'but.' When we are able to say 'I love you AND I am angry at you,' or 'I can grieve AND still feel happiness,' we embrace the wholeness of our being."

— Richard Boesch (contemporary)

"… the problem of therapy is to bring the 'head' into harmony with the energies that are informing the body so the transcendent energies can come through. Only when this occurs are you transparent to transcendence."

—Joseph Campbell (1904-1987)

"When I am working with a client in the therapy process, I bring my heart and soul fully to the present moment, as witness and fellow journeyer to their intrinsic truth and wholeness. Embedded storylines of self-criticism, shame, hurt and anger can be released as we experience our own basic goodness."

— Candida DeLuise (contemporary)

"Mindfulness-based Psychotherapy can help un-lock that inner wisdom you once knew—perhaps long before habits from implicit-learning built up biased filters and defensive armor that can cloud one's thinking. With mindful attention, kindness, and curiosity, psychotherapy can help inner wisdom flourish once again by removing any built-up obstacles to seeing yourself, others, and situations more clearly."

— William Harman (contemporary)

"To grieve is to love deeply. It is a cellular experience—one we feel in all of our senses. To bear witness to this grief as a therapist, friend, or family member is a gift beyond measure."

— Elizabeth Haase (contemporary)

"My husband David Spogen passed away twenty one years ago. But one day on a walk with my mother, I looked over at my 95 Suburban and said, "David is back." I guess this is all a matter of the

heart. When I designed David and my headstone, I chose this as my quote: 'Love from the heart lives forever.'"

— Rose Spogen (contemporary)

"Powerful change is possible when, together, client and therapist work to create and maintain a relationship where any/all feelings, thoughts, memories, hopes, physical perceptions, including aspects of self and experiences that may have been hidden due to self-judgment or shame, are invited to surface and are met and even welcomed—explored with kindness, compassion, and curiosity."

— Lisa Happ (contemporary)

"As a therapy patient, you need to be able to take some risks, sit with some pain and discomfort, and open yourself up to new possibilities. If you can do all of that, the sky's the limit."

— David Sternberg (contemporary)

"I think it's the relationship and particularly what develops in an analysis when the relationship between an analyst and analysand gets disrupted and repaired. This is where the therapeutic action takes place."

— Ernest Wolf (contemporary)

"The greatest tool we have as therapists is our empathy—allowing ourselves to feel what our clients are feeling and to be present to their internal worlds as best we can. Letting them know that we understand and accept their feelings (no matter how unacceptable they find them), especially given their individual histories and experiences, can be healing."

— Peggy Miller (contemporary)

"The patience of my mother and the humor of my father is what I bring to my patients. With them backing me, I can zone in with calmness on what the patient wants to tell me about themselves."

— Mary Orler (contemporary)

"The power that exists in listening and making space for someone to process and find their own way is profound."

— Tegan Peterson (contemporary)

"Everyone deserves forgiveness, including ourselves. Having compassion for ourselves enables us to love others more genuinely."

— Bernard Knight (contemporary)

"Talk to yourself as you would someone you love."

— Brene Brown (contemporary)

"My work with clients with AIDS during the 1980's and 1990's was 'heart and soul work.' I experienced the loving therapist's paradox. Sometimes I felt, 'Thank God I don't fall in love with all of them.' At other times I felt, 'If I ever lose my ability to fall in love, I should stop doing this work.'"

— Jody Reiss (contemporary)

"In the moment a traumatized client shares their experience with me, they experience someone more present to them than they are to themselves. They experience someone seeing the value and the good in them that is too unbearable or unacceptable for them to see. It is this felt sense of being fully known as seen by another that creates a sense of connection, safety and freedom from the demons."

— Jean Gearon (contemporary)

"In the early days of sobriety when folks feel as if they are caught in a violent storm, therapy can create a safe harbor where the client finds moments of peace and begins to steady the ship of their heart, mind, and life. This allows the healing process to begin."

— William Pullen (contemporary)

"As a therapist who specializes in assisting LGBTQI clients, I often hear Virginia Satir whispering into my ear; 'See, affirm, and believe in people until they are able to embrace and express their authentic selves.'"

— Donnie Conner (contemporary)

"I want to love you without clutching; appreciate you without judging; join you without invading…"

— Virginia Satir (1916-1988)

"Therapy all comes down to therapists helping people understand themselves better so that they can live authentic and meaningful lives."
— Edward Andrews (contemporary)

"One of our greatest challenges as therapists is to be confident enough in what we know about identity, intimacy, context, adaptation, and change while also knowing how much there is yet to be learned."
— Gary J. Raymond (contemporary)

"The most illuminating work of therapy is to claim our inner darkness rather than deny it or project it onto others. In so doing, we can hope to achieve wholeness, if not perfection, in our lives. We live our lives in light and shadow, each serving as a necessary background against which the other can be discerned. It's no accident that the name

'Lucifer' given to the Prince of Darkness means 'Bearer of the Light.'"
— Don Chamblee (contemporary)

"Today as never before it is important that human beings should not overlook the danger of the evil lurking within. It is unfortunately only too real...Psychology is an empirical science and deals with realities."
— Carl Jung (1875-1961)

"Understanding the core constructs of historical...trauma for individuals of African descent who present in counseling is an essential phase for developing counselor efficacy."
— Malik Aqueel Raheem and Kimberly A. Hart (contemporaries)

"... heterosexual individuals who examine their heterosexuality become aware of the privilege that accompanies that identity."
— Connie R. Matthews (contemporary)

"When I am centered in my wise self, I'm able to deeply connect to the notion that everyone is trying the best they can. There are also (far fewer) times when I'm strongly connected to the notion that everyone is an idiot. But then I'm reminded that I too am trying the best I can. And that self-compassion helps me get back to my wise self."
— Victoria Sylos-Labini (contemporary)

"Humor in the helping relationship can open channels of communication and build trust. Everyone loves to laugh. If the patient is relaxed, you can help them heal and cope."

— Mary George (contempary)

←————————————→

PART THREE
FINAL UNDERSTANDINGS

CHAPTER EIGHTEEN
WELLBEING AND ENERGY

QUESTION #18

Do you have any final ideas about how we can expand our sense of wellbeing and fuel our energy?

ANSWER #18

We are all confronted each and every day of our lives with rising and falling sensations, thoughts, and emotions, as well as with whatever the world gins up and tosses at us. At our best, we try to respond proactively to all of it. But sometimes we can't get negative phenomena to dissolve or change in ways we would like them to. In these cases, the tool of "disidentification" can be a great aid to our wellbeing. The Italian psychologist Piero Ferrucci describes disidentification as an act of using both our consciousness, and our will, to unlink ourselves from thoughts, emotions, and/or behaviors that have ceased to be healthy and helpful.

So whenever I get up in the morning on the wrong side of the bed, or whenever I feel overwhelmed, I try to remember that I have the choice to see my situation as a heavy burden that I am destined to carry throughout my day, or as a passing storm cloud that is not deep-down important to me. Realizing this, I immediately feel a little more personal power and a little more hope.

When we become introspective about how we have lived our lives, we can often make the most sense of what we've done or avoided in any particular case by asking, "Did I take this particular step to 'save myself,' or to 'become myself?'"

"Saving ourselves" is a choice we make based on ego needs such as avoiding perceived or real danger and/or enhancing our worldly status. "Becoming ourselves," on the other hand, is a choice we make that moves us closer to our vital center without over-regard for worldly consequences. (Human life being the complicated and multi-natured phenomenon that it is, some of our decisions are actually based on both.)

Coming to see that some of the unenlightened or hurtful decisions we've made were based on what we assumed we needed to do to avoid loss or ruin can help us steer away from self-shame, or from unforgiving regret, as well as provide us with an opportunity to rethink those assumptions.

When we understand that other decisions we've made were based on the noble human instinct to be true to our deepest self, we just might experience an inner-glow.

And then we can bolster ourselves at any moment of the day or night by doing a short "joy amplification meditation." To do this, sit or lie quietly and search for a memory of something pleasant, exciting or even thrilling that has happened to you during any period of your life. If a memory doesn't come up, imagine a wonderful or magical scene with you in it. As soon as you catch what you're looking for, double down on the emotion, locate it in you body, and let it fill you up. While the emotion will inevitably recede in time and be replaced by something else, you will have given yourself a little reminder of what you are capable of feeling on the positive side. And you will have given your neurons a chance to fire one additional time in the direction of pleasure and hope, thus creating more of a tendency for them to want to go there again. You can repeat the meditation whenever you wish.

QUESTIONS FOR THE READER

Can you identify a few thoughts, feelings, and/or behaviors from which you would like to dis-identify?

Do you carry regrets about past decisions you've made? Might they take on a different emotional hue if you begin to see them as "saving yourself?" Do you recognize times when you have clearly chosen to "become yourself?"

If you've tried the joy amplification meditation above, what is the "best" recollection your memory has given you to date?

CHAPTER NINETEEN

LIVING THIS MOMENT

QUESTION #19

What challenges in our world do you think most deserve our attention and efforts?

ANSWER #19

One way of thinking about the challenges of this moment of history is to note that our relationships are in dire need of mending. Devaluing people on the basis of gender, race, geography, education, social class, religion, age, and sexual orientation is rampant. When we devalue other human beings, or use them for our benefit with little regard for their own wellbeing, there is injury to the persons being victimized, for sure, but also a debasement of the perpetrator.

We are also in a toxic relationship with the earth itself. Animals, rivers, mountains and many of the other features of our planet are sorely challenged by human exploitation and pollution. Global warming that is caused by our barely controlled toxic emissions into the atmosphere is a threat to all life here.

Repairing our relationships with each other and with the earth will, I believe, require a conversion of heart on the part of a strong majority of us. We all have the capacity to fall into the fear and greed that leads to exploitation. We all have the obligation to work on righting ourselves and our relationships.

Spanish writer Antonio Machado (1875-1939) has been one of my favorite poets ever since a friend introduced him to me several decades ago. His life included some of the most trying events we humans can experience. He lost his young wife to death three years after they were married. He lived through a great political rift within his country that led to a civil war and his eventual exile to France. He died at the age of sixty-four. Out of his hard experience, he wrote luminous verse.

In his poem "The Wind, One Brilliant Day" (translated here from the Spanish), Machado speaks to the human degradation of the earth, but also to the human capacity for remorse.

THE WIND, ONE BRILLIANT DAY
The wind, one brilliant day, called
to my soul with an aroma of jasmine.
"In return for the aroma of my jasmine,
I'd like all the aroma of your roses."

"I have no roses; all the flowers
in my garden are dead."

"Well then, I'll take the withered petals
and the yellow leaves and the waters of the
fountain."

The wind left. And I wept. And I said to myself:
"What have you done with the garden that was
entrusted to you?"

The great American poet Walt Whitman (1819-1892) leads us past our grief to experience our power and see and seize the moment we are in:

LEAVES OF GRASS
"I have heard what the talkers are talking…the talk of the
beginning and the end,
But I do not talk of the beginning or the end.
There was never any more inception than there is now.
Nor any more youth or age than there is now;
And will never be any more perfection than there is now."

Despite the suffering of enslavement and, more recently, the indignities of ongoing racism, African-American orators and artists often graciously point us toward liberation and joy.

For instance, African-American spirituals are some of the most powerful statements of hope that humans have ever composed. "Down By The Riverside," sung in our day by an array of interpreters including Mahalia Jackson, Pete Seeger, and Louis Armstrong, is a splendid example of this genre. Become entranced by its rhythms and its repetitions. It will lead you out of a mindset of cautious self-protection into one of generosity of spirit.

DOWN BY THE RIVERSIDE
Gonna lay down my burden…down by the riverside,
Gonna lay down my sword and shield…down by the riverside,
Ain't gonna study war no more.

Gonna stick my sword in the golden sand…down by the riverside,
Gonna put on my long white robe…down by the riverside,
Ain't gonna study war no more.

Gonna put on my golden shoes…down by the riverside,
Gonna shake hands around the world, down by the riverside.
I ain't gonna study war no more…

A QUESTION FOR THE READER

What gifts do you, personally, bring to our great task of healing our relationships with each other and with the earth? (Don't be modest!)

CHAPTER TWENTY

WORDS FOR CONTEMPLATION III

QUESTION #20

What do psychological thinkers and psychotherapists whom you admire have to say about human possibilities in our era?

ANSWER # 20

(Remember to join only as many conversations at one sitting as you wish. Come back later for the rest.)

$\longleftarrow \longrightarrow$

"The word of the universe is 'balance.' We feel most alive when the body, mind, heart and spirit are in equilibrium. Like the universe fiercely opening and expanding at the moment of the Big Bang, we must open and expand ourselves to find the balance the universe is seeking. It's exciting to work with others on their own fierce journey."

— Tim Rogers (contemporary)

"When I dare to be powerful—to use my strength in the service of my vision—then it becomes less and less important whether I am afraid."

— Audre Lorde (1934-1992)

"The core of my personal journey in life has been to seek justice, love deeply, and make my life count personally and in society."

— Mary Jean Collins (contemporary)

"Well, I wasn't really eating, I wasn't sleeping well. I was kind of drowning in my grief when Speaker Pelosi asked me to become the lead impeachment manager...I felt that (she) threw me a lifeline, because that became sort of a salvation and sustenance for me..."

— Jamie Raskin (contemporary)

"Respect your opponents. Sometimes they might be right."

— Mike Mansfield (1903-2001)

"Paradoxically, we become stronger, more vital and more open as we realize the contradictions within ourselves."

— Jan Phillips (contemporary)

"And now it is covid, climate change, and the demons that have been let loose in the collective."

— Peggy DeCelle (contemporary)

"Peace-making is the way we face pressure in a world of opposites."

— Joan Chittester (contemporary)

"I have been creating a series of quilts to represent everyone in the country who has been lynched. I'm trying to bring memory forward. My hope is that my work will contribute to a conversation connecting these many lynchings to today's racial killings, especially of black boys and men in our streets."

— Lynda Tredway (contemporary)

"We all need to be makers, to help build a public conversation. To be good at that is a contribution to the larger whole."

Arlie Hochschild (contemporary)

"If you want to be a community organizer, you've got to get out into the neighborhood and meet the people."

— Sandra Schleinz (1945-2020)

←——————————→

"Whether I am a theist or atheist, I cannot be in the Yellowstone backcountry without experiencing its spiritual wonderfulness."
— Dwight Fleck (contemporary)

"As stewards of God's creation, we are called upon to make the earth a beautiful garden for the human family. When we destroy our forests, ravage our soil, and pollute our seas, we betray that noble calling."

— Pope Francis (contemporary)

←——————————→

"Spending time in nature is a profound source of joy and wonder for me. It's where I feel most centered and most whole, and where I find the most effortless connection to source/higher self and my own intuition."

— Kathy Patrick (contemporary)

My greatest benefits from being in nature come when I do volunteer trail maintenance. Whether I am working with my wife Steph, teaching others, or simply working alone, it give me a sense of quiet accomplishment to have made the outdoors more accessible to others."
— John Stacy

"When despair for the world grows in me…I come into the peace of wild things who do not tax their lives with forethought of grief. I come into the presence of still water."

— Wendell Berry (contemporary)

"The nuns who taught me as a boy planted the seed of mysticism in me. Quakerism has been my adult path of return to the mystical sense of being and behaving."

— Phil Favero (contemporary)

"To have a clear perception...that the universe is all of a piece and that one has a place in it---one is a part of it, one belongs in it—can be so profound and shaking an experience that it can change the person's character...forever after."

— Abraham Maslow (1908-1970)

"I know who I am through my creation of art. It is my ground. As I work, doubts as to how to proceed vanish. The work provides the space to move toward beauty, toward the unknown and the unseen. Both the pursuit and the discovery feed and sustain me. It is how I understand the world and my place in it."

— Regina DeLuise (contemporary)

"Music and art are intertwined in our lives together. As John Lee Hooker says in reference to a musical child, 'It's in him and it's gotta come out.' For Danny, blues players really know how to express feelings that cannot be said in words. Visual art, for me, too, gives me another voice. We feel that music, art, and the creative spirit are expressions of the soul. We wouldn't be whole without them. The arts are so vital to make the world whole, too, and possibly bring the world together."

— Peggy and Danny Lynn (contemporaries)

125

"A wise professor once told me that to teach is to embark on a love affair. Both teacher and student must bring to the relationship seriousness of purpose, hard work, and a willingness to listen and learn. Creating conditions of trust and engagement in a classroom always enhances the likelihood of long-term success."

— Judy Aaronson (contemporary)

"I was recently reminded by my daughter Jenny, a second grade teacher, of the deep down hopefulness of humans. The big windows of Jenny's classroom face out toward a nearby cemetery. Her students frequently witness funeral processions going by. They know that the cars escort the bodies of deceased persons who will be buried. Recently Jenny overheard a group of the little ones agreeing: "That person will be back out of the ground some day. Just like the flowers."

— Anne Collins (contemporary)

"Baby goats are one of the cutest animals out there, and it's really nice to expose people who visit our farm to the goats and to where they get their milk."

—Alice Orzechowski (contemporary)

"I contracted polio when I was two years old. The doctor who came to the house told my father and mother that I would not survive.

Somehow I understood what he was saying. Then the doctor told my parents that they could let my beloved collie Buck into the room to comfort me. As soon as Buck came to me and I was able to touch him, I decided that I was going to live."

— Madeline Bott Nesmith (1926-2021)

"*Our cat Cinnamon was very fond of Louise. When she died, he would sometimes sit near the front door, perhaps hoping that the missing person would come in. He grieved like this for awhile and then moved more toward people, seemingly trying to strengthen his connection with the rest of the world.*"

— Frank de Leeuw (contemporary)

⟵——————————⟶

"*I am a therapist, but as I do my work, I see my father, the pastor, in me. I check in on people. I go out to them, say hello, and ask how I can help, as he did.*"

— Jonathon Kirkendall (contemporary)

"*As a spiritual director, I've learned how vital it is to listen. I've come to know that it is important, like in being a therapist, to mainly give feedback to directees only on what you've heard from them directly.*"

— John Coleman (contemporary)

⟵——————————⟶

"Kindness matters. Children and adolescents value how they're treated. If a teacher is genuinely kind and caring, if a teacher doesn't disengage from a struggling student, the student will likely respond, even if that response isn't readily apparent, even if the teacher doesn't see quick results."

— Janet Jakusz Favero

"I realize that trying to say something 'helpful' to myself in a hard moment may not help. However I can offer myself compassion—simply by acknowledging to myself, 'This is hard…this really hurts…'"

— Christopher Wemple (contemporary)

"It is very clear that our very survival…depends upon the acts and kindness of so many people…"

— Piero Ferrucci (contemporary)

$\longleftrightarrow$

"Spiritual work entails imagining a different world—a sanctified, God-infused world, full of justice and righteousness—and then taking up a way of being that moves us into that reality."

— Heidi Mills (contemporary)

"You may envision realities that do not yet exist; a sea of possibilities, an ocean of wonder where imagination is fueled by passion and wisdom."

— Stephen Stein (contemporary)

"Human beings collaborate in evolutionary change. We rewrite our own neural networks, retrain our brains to think originally and non-dualistically. We update our own software through our intentions, meditations and actions."

— Jan Phillips (contemporary)

"Once you can accept that the universe is matter expanding into nothing that is something, wearing stripes with plaid comes easy."
— Albert Einstein (1879-1955)

"Life is like arriving late for a movie, having to figure out what was going on without bothering everybody with a lot of questions, and then being unexpectedly called away before you find out how it ends."
— Joseph Campbell (1904-1987)

"If the imagination is shackled, and nothing is described but what we see, seldom will anything truly great be produced in either Painting or Poetry."
— Thomas Cole (1801-1848)

129

Dear reader,

Would you now consider making yourself a co-contributor to this book by becoming Thomas Cole's partner in a final wisdom set of two? Could you add several lines of your own wisdom about becoming a healthy and involved human being right here under his quote?

Take heart from our inspiring painter and use your imagination! Use your own handwriting and finish up with your own wonderfully unique signature. (If you wish, eventually share what you write here with other readers and myself on the book website.)

FAREWELL

Well, dear reader, we have come to our moment of parting. Thank you for sticking with me through these pages.

When singer/songwriter and cultural icon Patti Smith (contemporary) accepted Bob Dylan's Nobel Prize in Literature for him in Stockholm in 2016, she sang his famous song "It's A Hard Rain A-gonna Fall." The king and queen of Sweden were in attendance, and Patti was backed by a magnificent symphony orchestra. All began well. But after singing one verse, Patti froze and couldn't vocalize her next lines. She recovered only after telling her audience how nervous she was and how sorry she was for the misstep. Then, when she began singing again, she gave a wonderful performance.

In a subsequent interview, Patti gave us a clue as to why, in the end, she sang so well and was so well received that day. She told her interviewer that her first and foremost goal in every performance is to get connected to the audience and stay connected to them rather than worrying about singing technically perfect music.

Similarly, I believe that my own resilience as a therapist over the past forty years has had more to do with my making and maintaining robust human connections rather than with offering theoretical or strategic brilliance. When I've inadvertently lapsed, my clients have usually forgiven me because of the strength of our bond.

I hope that you too, dear reader, will forgive yourself for your own inevitable missteps on your road to wholeness. Similarly to how Chief Plenty-Coups learned from the errors of both his friends and his foes, please find the learning in each one of your wrong turns, pause in reverence for your efforts, and then move forward again.

I hope that reading and contributing to "Forty Years In The Therapist's Chair" has given you a few extra provisions for your life's journey. Know that I care about you, even if from afar, and that I wish you a very successful and happy life.

Godspeed,

Doug Favero

BIBLIOGRAPHY

Marianne Brandon, "Sex Tech, Sex Robots and the Future of Hetero Intimacy." TZK Webinar, 2022

Joseph Campbell with Fraser Boa, "This Business of the Gods: In Conversation with Fraser Boa."
WINDROSE FILMS LTD., 1989

Kate DiCamillo, "For the Eight-Year-Old in You.' "On Being" broadcast interview with Krista Tippett, March 2022

Piero Ferrucci, "The Power of Kindness." Tarcher, 2005

Michael Hainey, "Ben Affleck on the Gift of Second Chances." Wall Street Journal Magazine article, December 1, 2021

Thich Nhat Hanh, "How To Fight." Parallax Press, 2017

Thomas R. Insel M.D., "Healing: Our Path from Mental Illness to Mental Health." Penguin Press, 2022.

Carl Jung, "The Essential Jung."
Princeton University Press, 1983

Jonathon Lear, "Radical Hope, Ethics In the Face of Cultural Devastation." Harvard University Press, 2006

Frank B. Linderman, "Plenty-Coups Chief Of The Crows." University of Nebraska Press, new edition, 2002

A.H.Maslow, "Religions, Values, and Peak-Experiences."
Viking Compass Books, 1970

Elizabeth Nyamayaro, "I Am A Girl From Africa, A Memoir."
Simon & Schuster, Inc., 2021

Jan Phillips, "Still On Fire: Field Notes From A Queer Mystic." Unity Books, 2021

Jeffrey Rediger M.D., "Cured." Flatiron Books, 2020

Jody Reiss, "Looking Back: AIDS Tales and Teachings." 2021

Carl Rogers, "On Becoming A Person: A Therapist's View of Psychotherapy." Mariner Books, 1961

Lynda Tredway, "History Teacher Sews Quilts to Honor Lynching Victims." Montgomery Advertiser video interview with Jack Gruber, December 19, 2018

Bessel van der Kolk, "Trauma, the Body, and 2021."
"On Being" broadcast interview with Krista Tippett, November 2021

Walt Whitman, "Leaves Of Grass."
Dover Thrift Editions, 2007

Images of works by artist/painter Thomas Cole:
The Voyage of Life: Youth, The Voyage of Life: Manhood, and *The Voyage of Life: Old Age,* provided courtesy of the National Gallery of Art, Washington D.C. USA